T0162815

About the Author

DIA JACKSON As an inspirational writer/author my idea for the book is to give a fiction feel as if you are reading a story but it is actually a true living testimony. God has birthed and gifted her with 14 years of a lifestyle of prayer as the mantle of intercession and prayer rest on her life for leadership, Apostles, Prophets,  Evangelist, Pastors, and Teachers the fivefold ministry. As well as family, friends and the lost.

As "Not without My Daughter" is the first published book of many that will follow this woman of God called for such a time as this. This articulate writer wanted to capture the mind, heart, and soul of "daughters" all over the word to let them know that the power of a praying 'mother" is something that will leave a lasting life time legacy that will effectively pass on from generation to generation and will be left in this earth.

Dia has ministered to many young girls and young ladies before this book on several other topics such as teen pregnancy, abstinence, keeping their virginity, being a born again virgin, STD"S, abortion and how it is very possible to hold out for marriage and the excitement in holding out whether for the first time or after being given a second chance or more than second chances, how to be happy, have fun, and be whole in being single and that there is no reason we should have to settle we don't have to and that there is a beauty in waiting, "It's Worth the Wait" what God has joined 'let no man put asunder"! God wants his people to stop putting his name on what's not him!.

From losing almost everything 1st from "material possessions" clothes, shoes, (and anyone that knows Dia Knows she loves shoes) cars, jobs, furniture, apartments, living from place to place living out of bags, losing friends, family and the most devastating of all a situation of a sister who was diagnosed with cancer who God healed through chemotheraphy and radiation treatment because his hand of grace and mercy was on her life, after praying and fasting her sister through, 5 months later her "mother" was diagnosed with cancer and 9 months later the death of her own 'mother" had caused her to feel she had hit rock bottom(which happens to be the name of the foundation of a close friend of hers' ministry that she does ministry with mobile to ALL with no discrimination as they minister full time called off their jobs to work for the Lord) building her way back up with the Lord's help and family to God be the Glory!!!

Dia resides with her daughter Shyla and her two grandchildren Jaiyon and Samiyah in the state of New Jersey.

"Not Without My Daughter"

A MOTHER'S PRAYER
A FAMILY'S DETERMINATION-
TO SEE A DAUGHTER SET FREE
AGAINST THE ODDS

Dia Jackson

authorHOUSE®

AuthorHouse™
1663 Liberty Drive
Bloomington, IN 47403
www.authorhouse.com
Phone: 1-800-839-8640

Published by AuthorHouse   08/31/2016

ISBN: 978-1-4634-4521-8 (e)
ISBN: 978-1-4634-3837-1 (sc)

Library of Congress Control Number: 2011913331

Print information available on the last page.

Any people depicted in stock imagery provided by Thinkstock are models, and such images are being used for illustrative purposes only. Certain stock imagery © Thinkstock.

This book is printed on acid-free paper.

Table of Contents

The Phase

The reason I decided to write this book in the content of a story and a phase was because it is a must read book for especially young girls awareness. The content is story form to keep the reader to read a story or testimony that is true but at the same time sending them a message just enough to encourage and inform. To tell how and where they can get help and more understanding outside of the book. It also gives them something to identify with and relate too also especially in the young girls because the behavior that is displayed in the book is what more so takes place in the young girls from young teens maybe 16 years old or so maybe even younger to young adults on the streets every single day out in the public even very much so in the school system. The phase part of it was because number one I knew that this was just a phase because I knew deep down inside about her, her personality/character and at this time of her life she was trying and exploring things that really was not her. She was trying to be a follower and get acceptance, validation which would not last because she is a leader. So because she was unhappy about many things she was trying many things and she never ever seemed happy or comfortable in what she was doing. It was almost like something to be doing or trying maybe because somebody did it. Phases don't last because we get tired of them and sometime they wear us out and it is time to move on to the phase of my life. If it was truly happiness it would not have been so much chaos and drama continuously. So I knew it was phase for her to go through that would make her strong and point her to her real dreams, goals and desires not someone else's what they want or are doing. Secondly, I chose phases instead of chapters because with chapters you have to give a lot of information and they are much longer than to take the reader through steps or phases of the events but still give an effect like chapters in their completeness. So for a book a first book I wanted it to be short and a small soft cover that you could hand carry in your book bag or pocketbook, if you don't like a lot of reading or don't want to much information you would have that, for a mother or grandmother who don't do or like a lot of reading or you just maybe don't have a lot of time this would be good. In conclusion telling some the phases in short because are just some there were more but these would hopefully be a help to get through the phases. Webster dictionary defines the word:

> **phase** 1: a particular appearance or state in a regularly recurring cycle of changes <phase of the moon>

Dedication

This book is dedicated to three very dear and close to my heart people who inspire no matter what my one and only beloved daughter Shyla Shan'e Jackson. At the age of 3 I realized you were a gift to me and this world from God. God has placed so many precious gifts and talents in you for his glory and his kingdom. Your life is in the palm of the master 's hand. "I love you Shy aka "Muk".

To my grandson Jaiyon Malachi Jackson "you are Jesus boy". Tamela Davis aka Tam my partner all I can say is girl you know this one was roughest thus far. I remember the day I called you to check on you in the hospital and you were ready to get up and go a "mission" as we often did because you knew it was only a mission but not impossible "rest in glory" when things get rough I think how you would say "Chic" and I knew the push the encouragement was coming miss you much!

Acknowledgements

1ST and foremost I give all praise, credit, and glory to God, God 1st for without his Holy Spirit living in me I would have never thought I could even write a book. Thank you Holy Spirit for getting this published.

I thank God for the best parents in the world George and the late Elaine Jackson mommy('rest in glory") I miss you sooo much and I know you knew that I would do it even though your not here to read it (forever your babygirl) mommy, daddy you both always see and saw sooooo much in me all my life and always think and believe that I can do anything. "Love you both".

My one and only big brother Dwaine Jackson I love you dearly, thank you for "your own personal nickname" you gave me when I was little that no one knows, aside from my family nickname, thanks for the time when I was little and mommy was gone beat me and you picked me up and took me in your room and locked mommy out..lol!.

My two pretty beautiful sisters/confidant/friend, Debra Jones Jackson and Dena Hawkins. You are both my role models, we will always be " 3 the hardway". A threefold cord is not easily broken I love you both so much.

To my nephew Jakai Jaquan Hawkins thank you for

believing your auntie can do it, as you often tell me "you can do it auntie". Auntie love you Kai.

Prophetess Niambi Brice Ni "It takes one to know one" Evangelist Tan "somebody on this prayer line need to start back writing"lol.. Evangelist Sakinah-this is what we do, "we write it down" Pastor Tawana the text"start back writing Dia" Pastor Pattie anointed woman of God, Romans 8:38 you prayed from the night of & you did not stop, when I felt all alone and all crazy Pastor Ebony and aunt Rhee all I heard was all I see is her coming out and when I wanted to waver yall never did and then anointing oil was slapped everywhere over me ☺, Prophetess Dionne Price your prayers of encouragement and saying I believe God "I love y'all all for real, y'all some hard no nonsense preachers JESUS!!! YEARS of pushing and crushing that yall put on a sista for real, through the preaching, teaching, praying, prophesying, counseling &rebukes many mornings, days, and nights of tears Lord have mercy from all y'all in different ways were hard on me OMG but y'all all wrapped it up with real smooth love that I was able to only stand because I knew it was Him the HOLY GHOST through all of you lol.

Pastor Ronald Jones thank you for who you are, you are very dear to my heart and I appreciate you for appreciating me for who I am in God. Pastor Tracy Davis, my sister and my secret ear when I called, came by, or spent the night no matter what the time or day you were that ear. Last but not least Pastor Emma Salter I am eternally greatful for 14yrs of impartation I will always love you deeply.

Introduction

This book is a book of determination, faith, and hope-it first speaks to a mother, a father who has a 'daughter' in a lesbian life style but further it speaks to (a son in homosexuality . There may be a sister, brother, grandmother, or any family member or friend who has been praying for someone in it or you may be the person involved in it. It speaks to all those all over the world not just in the church and you want to see them "set free'. Especially those in the Christian faith that have been holding on to see their child come out of this life style for years. However this book is by no means written to condemn, criticize, or judge anyone Jesus said you shall know the truth and the truth shall make you free. Only once truth is revealed can a lie be exposed and seen as a lie because most of the time lies are covered or hidden.

> And you shall know the truth, and the truth shall make you free."(John 8:32 NKJV).

> Therefore if the Son makes you free, you shall be free indeed."(John 8:36 NKJV).

Jesus himself was anointed of God to heal brokenness, deliver the captivity of, and set at liberty (freedom) to those who have been oppressed by this life style of demise (homosexuality).

> "The Spirit of the LORD is upon Me,
> Because He has anointed Me
> To preach the gospel to the poor;
> He has sent Me *to heal the brokenhearted,
> To proclaim liberty to the captives
> And recovery of sight to the blind,
> To set at liberty those who are oppressed;
> (Luke 4:18 NKJV).

The world we live in today in the earth realm, in the natural sense of things strongly base their living according to freedom of rights and speech, it's a free country. " It's your thing do what you wanna do". We regard mans law and we should obey mans law, but what about respecting God's law, his principles, and his order? The reality is this, what we do and how we live now, that is what will determine our ultimate eternal end, with God's son, Jesus Christ being the judge of it all. However, many people in this world choose to not obey God's law because they would rather obey what is in the natural and what can be seen in front of us for right now. Do we see the air?, or our breath?, no, but we know it exist because we are breathing. It seems that the spiritual does not matter much to the lesbian/homosexual who says "I was born this way" this is an incorrect way of thinking. The bible proves this controversy is of no "truth" and offers a way out for this corrupt thinking and corruptible seed that has been planted in your mind. As I speak to you through God's word and this book, You can be born again and get understanding from God's word to help you and heal you from this misconception. Yes God does love everybody, he loves the homosexual & lesbian, and so do I but those that practice this lifestyle will not have eternal life with God but will be separated from God in the end of this life just as any other sin we cannot separate pick and choose and we cannot be deceived.

> Jesus answered and said to him, "Most assuredly, I say to you, unless one is born again, he cannot see the kingdom of God." (John 3:3 NKJV).

> Wisdom *is* the principal thing;
> *Therefore* get wisdom.
> And in all your getting, get understanding.
> (Prov 4:7)

> having been born again, not of corruptible seed but incorruptible, through the word of God which lives and abides *forever (I Pet 1:23).

The book your about to read is not a book to bash, hurt, harm or portray a hate crime against the lesbian/homosexual lifestyle, no that is not the message my heart would never let me do that because God love is in me, but it is to convey the Love of God for them. God does love the person in this lifestyle (and again I do too I must say this emphatically) but he also wants you "OUT" and you can heal, love and live again just like with any other relationship or addiction that is difficult and hard to get over. God is a divine intervention in the impossible, against the odds, and he specializes in the miraculous because you are special. The bible speaks and declares very clearly in Genesis the 19th chapter of how God destroyed a city because of this "wicked" act. Not the person is wicked but the act is. God even used a man by the name of Abraham to plead for the city in the chapter before if they would turn from this grievous sin. (Genesis 18: 20-33 KJV). God still does today in 2011 offers and a way "OUT" of this lifestyle if you want out, and to understand that if you don't want out there is a way that seems right or might I add even feels right(I quote: "How does something that feels so right, be wrong" Shyla Shane' Jackson) but the end of that thing is destruction for further understanding reading is found in Romans chapter 1 also read more on this later in the book.

A family's life of a lived journey of a devastating, raging battles, a nightmare that actually came true.

I had to stay determined, keep the faith, and not give up hope. Take the journey with me. This book is scripturally based but the contents and wording of the book is of the actual events that took place in the form a storyline, except it is not fictional it is an absolute actuality, reality of a chain of events.

Special Thanks

Once again and as I will probably repeat throughout this book thank you Lord for without you this could no way be possible for me. I will never forget our first date when you filled me, the gift and present of your Holy Spirit on February 28, 1997 at 2am, it was the greatest moment in my life that I will never forget and I was never the same from that moment. God I thank you for all the times that you would come to me in the Spirit and quietly touch my heart and encourage me keep writing when I was discouraged, how when I would be encouraged and you would just flow through and touch my fingers and I would type as a typist taking a typing test as I heard you downloading in my mind what you wanted me to say. There were times when financially I would get discouraged but you provide the finance it was some delays but not denied, there were times when I would make excuses of why I wasn't getting it done and you would send literally countless people women and men to say to me when you gone do your book. I remember someone I would never expect to ask me about my book said to me don't make me find a publisher for you, you used whom you would out of the unexpected that's just how amazing you are. I thank you most of all for defeating the biggest giant of discouragement that came up against me which was fear of rejection from writing this type of book in this day and time but I also will remember you were loving but you were adamant when you said to me I have made you to be an "controversial woman" everything that you are I already made you that before you were born and formed you in your mother's womb. So all that you thought you would cause as a stir and why would you be stirring things up like that, it wasn't I but you let me know it is you not me and anytime you want something to get across, you will cause a writer to write it down and make it plain that others would read it and know . You have called me to write and speak not be to silent on things that I have specifically experienced and live out through your alive written word.

Lord I am truly always and forever yours.

Phase 1
Suspicions

What do you do when you find out that your suspicions about your child's behavior have become a reality? What do you do when your most inner thoughts and feelings are confirmed to be true? What do you do when living a life as a Christian and raising your child in a Christian home, and like brother Job in the bible the thing that you feared the most has come upon you. " For the thing I greatly feared has come upon me, and that which I was afraid of has come unto me. "Mother" felt like she had gotten hit with a ton of bricks. Mothers you know how it is, they say it's intuition of a woman, you know the gut feeling type of thing. Eventually "mother" began to see the signs and the suspicion was right there surfacing more and more because as woman we tend to want the proof behind what we already feel or know but we just want that proof we just wanna feel like okay now I know because I saw it for myself. "Daughter" always talked about it her sophomore year in High School as a matter of fact no it was freshman year, but it was always the "other girls" that were doing it. She said it was disgusting!!. It was always guess whos? Gay, so and so. Then there was always the "late night" phone call and always of the same sex. Yeah, what you do in the dark always comes to the light. The calls were always quiet, discreet, and very sneaky, you know the DL creeping stuff gotta be late night like in the dark, think you hiding, it's a secret going. This is usually a very common way how the devil moves in on his victims the bible says he was the most subtle than any beast of the field which the Lord God had made. (Gen 3:1-6, KJV). As 'mother" confronted the late night calls the response was there's nothing going on she's just a friend and "I'm not into that"(denial). The devil was setting a trap. Time went on and attending after school pep rallies and basketball games became more than "cheering go team go slam dunks and hoops". In all actuality it was sneaking behind the bleachers, you know doing sneaky things. The game's been over "where were you and who were you with it was always my girlfriend like a this my girl or a male friend or a girlfriend who had a boyfriend to throw things off. Did you know so and so has a boyfriend now, but none of the boys are attracted to me why is that, what's up with that. This was all a cover up and another excuse. Sin always wants to be covered and hid but the bible says your sin will find you out, "But if you will not do so, behold, you have sinned against the Lord; and be sure your sin will find you out" (Num 32:23, AMP). Sin also has a way of getting someone else involved Genesis 3:6-10, the 6th verse in this chapter shows sin is also contagious look how the woman gave also to her husband and he did eat. Let's pause and think here for a minute, when you are in a lesbian/homosexual lifestyle I believe someone, somehow, or some way you were introduced to this lifestyle like with anything . It could have been a misfortune of an event, a violation of your person, a rape, a molestation, a television program, a movie, internet, a book, a conversation, a thought, a broken marriage, a break up, low self-steem, or a friend. This list can go on and on. Whatever the entry point or introduction whether so called good or bitter because it was bad there was an open door of a vulnerability period in your life for the devil, and he took advantage of a sensitive situation, a painful experience or series of painful events. As "mother" began to search for more clues, through book bags, dresser drawers, pant pockets, under mattresses etc... Don't go snooping, do I see what I think I see? Valentine's Day card from the same sex inappropriate wording, pictures, and "rainbow" name tags representation of the gay community.

I am not bashing the gay community but gotta move on. Oh no I'm just kidding around, "daughter" would say I am not serious about this I'm just playing, don't play with fire because you just might get burned, an open door to the devil is an open opportunity. "Neither give place to the devil", (Ephesians 4:27. KJV). Suspicions were coming to a head and about to burst it was more like facing the facts now. God had gifted "daughter" to sing and write songs and singing in the church "mother" thought that would keep "daughter" on the right path. Well one day "daughter" decides to sing in the school choir and make demos after school going to the studio, music was always in her heart but the devil needed a way to use what you like for a set up or an excuse "set up" followed by deception. "Daughter" decides to prove her not involvement by asking "mother" if she could help her witness about Jesus to her friends that were lesbians, "daughter knew if she could throw "mother" off the track or the trail she would still be covered. Question, How can all your friends be doing this but not you? You are known by your association you are not who you associate with but you will be known by your associations does "mother" have dumb dumb on her forehead. Does birds of a feather still flock together? Still, no, not me "daughter" would say. "Mother" finally one day met with one girl friend let's call her Tiffany. "Daughter" never wanted "mother" to meet any of her outside of the church friends. "Mother" met Tiffany and prayed for Tiffany and read the word of God to her. I know its wrong Tiffany said my mom told me so also. Tiffany said I learned it was wrong in church also, I use to go to church but it was still hard to get out it was to difficult. "Mother" assured Tiffany with God nothing is impossible even though it may be hard but it can be done if you want it bad enough. (Matthew 19:26). With men this is impossible; but with God all things are possible. Tiffany did not confess Christ that day. "Mother" still under the assumption of a suspicion with "daughter" still saying "not me". One morning at 12am the house phone rang not "daughter's cell phone" Tiffany was hospitalized for drunkenness because of the amount of alcohol consumption her body had consumed because of a break up from a lesbian relationship. She had passed out and she had an asthma attack. "Mother" had never met Tiffany's mother before and it was Tiffany's mother was on the other end of the phone distraught and pleading for "mother" to come pray for Tiffany, wow things a mother will do for her "daughter". "Mother" got dressed and headed to the hospital in the dark rainy night hardly able to see through the darkness with "daughter" sitting in the passenger's seat. The drive was quiet as "Mother" began praying in the car. The strange thing looking hind sight "daughter" joined in the prayer praying in agreement. Upon arrival to hospital the hospital room wreaked of alcohol very strong as Tiffany layed in the bed slumped over, her mom on one side of the bed, and mom's boyfriend on the other side as they yelled back and forth to one another. I believe Tiffany's mom was getting him to stop all the cussing he was doing as "Mother" stayed focused. Everyone greeted one another except Tiffany she was to out of it pass drunk, as Tiffany's mom continued to shush her boyfriend and asked "mother" to pray. This time "mother" offered Christ to Tiffany "mother" told her Jesus could forgive her of all her sins and deliver her from lesbianism as "daughter" stood on the other side of the bed shaking her head up and down in a yes he can motion. As Tiffany sluggishly crabbed for "mother's" and "daughter's' hands she repented of her sins and confessed with her mouth Jesus as Lord. "That if thou will confess with thy mouth the Lord Jesus, and shalt believe in thine heart that God has raised him from the dead, thou shalt be saved. For with the heart man believeth unto righteousness; and with the mouth confession is made unto salvation" (Romans 10:9-10 KJV).

Immediately as the prayer ended and everyone opened their eyes God had performed a miracle Tiffany's once bloodshot red eyes that were red when "mother and daughter approached Tiffany and barely open were instantly as he Jesus saved her washed away her sins with his blood instantly her eyes were no longer red and her eyes were wide open, her speech was back to normal, and she sat up in the hospital bed. Woww what a in an instant moment. Tiffany's mom was amazed as the hospital room was filled with God's presence. Glory to God!!! Tiffany's mom shouted to her boyfriend shut up!!! Be quiet !!! man, do you see what God just did he performed a miracle look at her eyes, look how the redness is gone and she is sitting up and speaking normal, with excitement Tiffany's mom continued, please be quiet or leave the room don't you see God is at work, man!!! "Mother's" heart was filled with joy as they all rejoiced and heaven was rejoicing over one sinner that came to repentenance. "I say unto you, that likewise joy shall be in heaven over one sinner that repenteth, more than over ninety and nine just persons, which need no repentance"(Luke 15:7 KJV).Halleulah glory and praise be to God. This showed the devil that God could and did touch the heart of a lesbian let me pause and say this the same can be true for your son mother. They can change through the power of God. However, as "mother" rejoiced for this this girl, not knowing in the same room that this miracle took place in her very own "daughter" was in denial, but after the miracle took place the suspicion was gone while Tiffany's mom was still yelling God is working, be quiet and let God work!!!!!!

5

Phase 2
* Facing the Facts *

High School was coming to an end for the year and it was time to go to the prom. Although "mother" wanted the facts, facing them would be something different. No one wants to face what's really going to hurt them in the interim. First your going to the prom then your not going, back and forth, back and forth, then final decision, "daughter" was going to go and the preparations began. Getting ready was not to bad with the exception that "daughter" wanted a dress she saw in a magazine on a very famous R&B singer however "mother" could not let you reveal your entire body like that you gotta be kidding me, how about a little bit of a leg, not to much, sleeve less but that's gone cut it. "Mother" went to meet the prom date and his mom and things went smooth although prom date mom was a little rough around the edges. Not a problem for "mother" after all "mother" has a past, let's just say that, about that. The day arrives and the day was nice and partly sunny, the streets were crowed with limos all over, due to the fact that more than one prom was going on that day. As the limo arrived and everyone was around taking pictures, cam recorders, cell phones pictures and some of prom date mom and her family were tripping really hard. Get closer, do this and do that, as they laughed out loud and yelling out prom dates name, oh no, "mother" was not having that, okay let's have fun and enjoy the day but calm it down a bit gee whiz. Let them take the picture like a lady and a gentleman, not like "Bonnie and Cldye". Can it get any wilder? Off to the toast off as the jammed packed cars, limos, and the prom candidates, family and friends, crowed the High School courtyard to see them off. Oh my, half naked young girls are all over the courtyard showing just about everything, maybe just one young lady did have a shawl on of course everybody thought she was corny. She was probably the church girl or the quiet one that everyone picked on. Suddenly, out of the crowd there appears this young girl dressed like a young boy not going to the prom but lurking in the crowd calling out "daughters" name. One of "mothers" sisters began to follow the young lady as she disappears in the crowd. That is exactly what the devil do show up then gone with the wind just like that he rears his head and then discreetly he's out "Daughter" was busy caught up in the moment of pictures and moving around and she loves the camera too she was here and there she probably never even noticed or heard any of it. This is just like the devil also trying to copy God which he could never do. Just as God has a plan for life your life "For I know the thoughts that I think toward you, Saith the LORD, thoughts of peace, and not of evil, to give you an expected end" (Jeremiah 29:11 KJV). God's plan for all people is always good but the devil is always out to kill, steal, and destroy God's perfect way. "The thief cometh not, but for to steal, and to kill, and to destroy: I am come that they might have life, and that they might have it more abundantly" (John 10:10, KJV).

The time was passing by in the night and as a mother would do "mother" surely was not going to go to bed until "daughter" got in even if she slept with one eye open. Well as in most cases after the prom ends no one ever wants to go straight home especially if you have other plans of doing something you have no business doing more than likely. "Is that one of the facts".? Once again as "daughter" often did she was past her curfew time, whattttt, curfew time what is that maybe that was back in the day in your time. No one has a curfew now, Oh yes they do, because your one and you do. Finally the key is in the door, a sigh of relief but a little agitated, its 4am or 5am Do you know where your child is? Forget channel 5 fox saying its 10pm do you know? "Mother" should have called Fox Five news personally and said no I really don't to be honest. So how was the prom first and secondly why are you coming in at this hour? Oh it was okay, not all that, well I'm a little late because bla bla bla yeah okay once again you didn't come in on time, yeah I know, I'm sorry my bad as the young people would often say.

Graduation day came and "mother" was glad after hearing so many stories of all the lesbians in "daughters" school "mother" was glad for her to be leaving that school. It seemed like the whole school was full of this lifestyle, "mother" went to school for "daughter" one day and the hallways and the cafeteria was crowed with girls dressed like boys some of the girls "mother" thought were boys for real it was so sad and heartbreaking to see many pretty girls looking like boys OMG. So graduation day was a delightful day with the family and friends and no sign of the facts of the reality had come as yet. So okay maybe it was just the school setting or environment just the regular school pressure from peers in school. As the summer approached things began to mount up one after another like evidence building up some kind of case or trial all "daughters" friends were lesbians with the exception of maybe just that one again. As "mother" again confronted "daughter" just like in High School days why you never let "mother" meet your friends or their mothers you never bring them around. Who does that? No parent meets their friend's mother anymore that's played out, what okay I'm just stupid is and stupid does like Forrest Gump and no "mother" you won't approve of my friends. Why not? Well I don't know to avoid an arguing maybe you will I'll bring them around okay mommy just so you will feel comfortable. Yes, that would be nice. Of course it never happened and the late nights of coming in missing curfew still continued. One day "mother" searched "daughters" cell phone to find so many phone numbers in one cell phone, ghee whiz, names majority girls and some code names that seemed to be boys but they were really girls.

"Your getting warmer"

Eventually, "mother" felt she was getting closer to the facts "daughter" was hanging with a couple of other girls whose names she had never heard before and surely she had never met them. "Daughter" was rebelling more and more not meeting curfews became gross, and stating I'm 18 does'nt that mean I'm grown. I should 'nt have a curfew, oh no sweetie you don't have your own place, you have no job to pay any bills, and your not financially independent. Shortly after this conversation "mother" has a dream regarding "daughter" that satan is desiring to have her that he may sift you as wheat "And the Lord said, Simon, Simon, behold, Satan hath desired to have you, that he may sift you as wheat: (Luke 22:31 KJV). "Daughter" could not at this time see or receive this warning. There is always a warning, remember God never destroy a city without a warning and he always makes a way of escape, nothing just happens. "Daughter" got so mad and hostile with "mother" and then the bomb dropped". I have had one experience with one girl one time in that lifestyle but it's over, but I believe that's how I am, because boys are not interested in me.

This was far from the truth "mother" knew this but the devil had already planted this seed in "daughters" mind. This was all going in a direction "mother" was not feeling comfortable with, very shortly after the first experience came and went, followed by another experience and before long there was nothing but this friend of a friend of a friend, and so on and so on, this was annoying mother so much all this friend of a friend stuff and they all were girls into the lifestyle. They were always spending much time together. Was this a fad? That would pass, Is this some sort of game their playing? Absolutely not the case the devil wants to pull you in and accuse you as being guilty before God. "And I heard a loud voice saying in heaven, Now is come salvation, and strength, and the Kingdom of our God, and the power of his Christ: for the accuser of the brethren is cast down, which accused them before God day and night"(Revelation 12:10, KJV). How can you be a christian, a child of God involved in this lifestyle? This is the reason satan wants to web the child of God into this way of living because of their salvation, their strength that comes from God and the Kindgom of God that has come into their life this brings them the power of Jesus Christ in their life to resist this way of thinking and living. Therefore, the accuser Lucifer himself, who was fallen and cast out of heaven (Isaiah 4: 12 KJV, "How art thou fallen from heaven, O Lucifer, son of the morning! how art thou cut down to the ground, which didst weaken the nations!") He wants the same for the child of God he lost his place so he wants you to lose your place or never gain your place in heaven. So if he think he can get you before you really get saved not just go to church but read the bible and get the word and get understanding on it he got you, but no because God is going to give everyone the chance to hear know and choose there is always a way choose the right way now and not be sorry later. So he the devil deceives and accuses the child of God to God once he's roped you in he is very good at that. "Daughter" was not seeing this at all because of the blinders that covered her eyes. Summer is here and "mother" was not looking forward to the drama that would come with the hot weather. Graduation was over and the drama continued but then there were times when "daughter" would come to "mother" and say I want to bring some of the girls to you to introduce them to Christ, but again it was always "them" but not "me". One or two might show up and the other would not show up. These were girls who were not happy, they were confused, in despair, had been hurt by boys, had been molested, raped, abandoned by fathers, neglected by mothers, dysfunctional homes and the list was just endless. Yet God is still faithful and always offers a way of escape from all of the above, there is a "way out". Although life has been, is, and will be hard and can have devastating events God does want to help you when you hurt. "Come unto me, all (ye) that labour and are heavy laden, and I will give you rest. Take my yoke upon you, and learn of me; for I am meek and lowly in heart: and ye shall find rest unto your souls. For my yoke (is) easy, and my burden is light"(Matthew 11: 28-30 KJV). "But remember that the temptations that come into your life are no different from what others experience. God is faithful he will keep the temptation from becoming so strong that you can't stand up against it. When you are tempted, he will show you a way out so you that you will not give into it"(I Corinthian 10:13, NLT).

College life began at the end of August and "daughter" said maybe getting away from the environment and focusing on college life will help me get myself together. College life was going good, "daughter" had met new friends and guess what mommy "daughter" would say some of them are Christians and we are going to begin a on campus bible study to try to draw the ones who not christians "wow!!! This is great. Things were going well, classes were interesting, studying was good, good grades were in the making, and the bible study groups were going well some boys were even interested and the talks about Christ was encouraging. Ring, hello, "mother" answer the phone, on the other end "daughter" guess who goes to my school one of the girls from up the way who was into the lifestyle. Well, I tried to witness to her "daughter" said, but she does not want to change her lifestyle so I'm going to keep my distant with her, well okay gotta go need to go to class, talk to you later, love ya. "Wherefore come out from among them, and be ye separate, saith the Lord, and touch not the unclean(thing): and I will receive you, And will be a Father unto, and ye shall be my sons and daughters, saith the Lord Almighty"(II Corinthians 6: 17-18, KJV). God wants to be a father to his sons and daughters who want to come out from among them. "Is it everywhere"? looking hind site on the day of orientation parents were able to stay the weekend on campus but unable to stay in the same room with their child. The students had to stay in a room with another student to get the feel of having a room mate, freshman's could not have a room alone. While waiting in line to get the key for the room and look on the list to see who would be "daughters" weekend room mate in front of "mother" was a young lady dressed like a boy and she even looked like a boy, "mother" said to herself "Is it everywhere you go? That pretty beautiful girls everywhere are changing their beauty their looks to look like a boy "a dude" oh no this just can't be. Later that night while "mother" was in her room "daughter" came to visit and talk about the tour of the campus and the people she had met. "Mother" asked had she met her room mate, no not yet, she still has not come to the room but her belongings are there but we have not met. With much excitement!!!

"daughter" left the room kissed "mother" and said I'll be back to visit before we turn in for the night after I finish touring the campus and meeting the other students. Hours later as the late night approached "daughter" came back still full of excitement about the campus and having fun with the people she had met that were really nice people and from so many different states, she thought that was cool. She wanted to go out to get something to eat so we drove out to the spot where the college kids hung out and went to eat. While out eating "daughter" says oh yeah I met my room mate, remember the girl and this is exactly how "daughter" said it you, the one that was in front of you in line when we were signing in and getting the key. Yeah her, but she don't talk much and she doesn't stay in the room to much we just kind of said hi and said where we were from and that was it. "Mother" was uncomfortable once again but what could "mother" do you can't hate on people because of this lifestyle because the world excepts it as its okay but at the same time you don't want to except it as a christian because God doesn't but love must be given and shown through the power of God's anointing we must always walk in love and truth. You just pray and hope for deliverance, not just for your "daughter" but someone else's as well, after all she's somebody's "daughter" and how can the lost be found if we don't help them someone helped us when we were lost. The night was sleepless looking out the window at the moon, thinking and wondering if "daughter" was okay along with "mother" hates sleeping in strange places and strange beds but "mother" tried to lay down and rest. When all of a sudden "mother" feels in her heart "daughter" is not sleep either. Within minutes there was a knock on the outer door and some other parent opened the outer door.

"Mother" sat up in bed, waiting for the knock at her room door. Knock, knock, it's me ma, "daughter" said. I can't sleep she said. Does it have anything to do with the room mate situation, well, yes and plus I have a "confession" to make. No, not a confession "mother" thought I'm already not wanting to face the facts as it is please don't say what I know your gone say but I still don't wanna hear it. "Daughter" began to say how it was a struggle that she was back involved in this lifestyle but wanted to use college as a way to get away thinking maybe another environment might help it might help to meet new people, "mother" assured her that that would not take it away, you know what will get you out "mother" said. We talked and talked and then ended in prayer. The weekend was over we headed back home preparing for until it was time to leave again weeks later for the real deal. It was kind of quiet back on the home front not to much going on things were just low key. The day to leave came for school and on our way we went, the drive was long but a lot of fun, jokes and hiking as the family often do, food, and laughter with the family felt good. We signed in got the keys and to our surprise the roommate didn't show up or had decided not to attend the college and "daughter" would be have a different roommate so maybe this was better for "daughter" since her previous roommate was into the that lifestyle and this could be a problem for "daughter" after all she had just spoke with "mother" how she wanted to try to stay strong to overcome any temptations. We were on our way to meet the new roommate low and behold only to get to the room and find that the new roommate parent was into an open lesbian relationship. Okayyyyy, "mother" and family thought, no offense but maybe room mates mom and friend won't visit much, once again what could "mother" do or the family but once again pray truth be told this was just adding people to the prayer as "mother" was praying for "daughter" now there are others that would need prayer . We were nice and pleasant so were they we unpacked, set up, got situated, prayed and we hugged and kissed and were on our way.

Believe it or not no one cried if so we hid our tears from each other. On the way home "mother" wanted to several times say stop the car lets go back "daughter" can't go to that school but "mother" was not in control God was. As weeks passed roommates mom and friend visited often after all they lived in the state so they dropped in very frequently. "Daughter" called a lot and sent emails all the time. Then one day at work "mother" received a call from "daughter" saying I tried to call you last night to ask for the pastor's phone number to get some scriptures for this all night prayer we had in my dorm. It was myself and another young lady who headed it who is strong in her faith, you know the one I told you about. "Daughter" had right away met this young lady after the family had left and the students were getting to know other students in the dorm. When they started the prayer a couple of the other girls were there and of course the topic of discussion was homosexuality. It really went well "daughter" said one girl got a breakthrough as she excepted Christ. God really used me and the other Christian girl to pray for them and we stayed up all night we could not sleep the spirit of God was really in the room. No one wanted to leave the room as we all cried and praised God. As a mother I did not know what to believe because of the distance and previous times of having hope that this was it and then bammmm!!! It's here again, she would tell me one thing and I would believe her and then I would find out it was not how she really said or she just kept falling back into it. "Daughter" was saying mommy I promise you I'm staying strong but a "mother" knows her child or does she? The inside of me was not at rest and I had this queezy feeling in the pit of my stomache.

Just that quick after this so called experience with prayer and God or maybe it was a true experience. The phone calls and the emails got less and less, grades were not looking good, and problems with the roommate already, or was 'daughter" on the up and up. Upon arrival to the school "daughter" is packed and surely ready to go while "mothers" dream of her daughters College Graduation day goes down the drain. "Daughter" calls for her friend and everyone heads to the car while in "mothers" mind the wheels are turning saying I can't believe this after several, several trips on the weekends to the college for visits, pop ups or expected, things seemly to have working and going well, believing college life would help her get focused but yet she wasn't focused at all. Not on school at least and to top things off there would be another trip to get the remaining of her belongings. Also knowing weeks later there would be a return trip in a van to get the heavier belongings that were placed in storage was annoying mother" along with not understand how did things go from wanting to be there to wanting to leave and come home . On the drive home "mother" talks with the friend about school, was only coming home for the weekend, she talked about where she was from, what she likes to do, and a little bit of church, because all of "daughter" friends referred to "daughters" mother as is your mother a preacher or if they see "mother" where is your mother at church. As we rode and continued to talk "daughter" sits in the passenger incognito with a big grey hooded sweater with the hood on head and her face toward the window barely saying anything. After driving for an hour or so its time to stop for of course get something to eat before the car is barely parked "daughter" takes off and walks ahead of "mother" and friend. Well wow what in the whirl wind was that all about too! "Mother" and friend continue walking and talking entered the restaurant to eat and "daughter" was out of sight. Then suddenly as a rushing mighty wind I mean "daughter" was so quick and speedy out of a sudden. So "daughter" comes out of the bathroom incognito as "mother" says what would you the problem. Unbeknown to me the room mate is gone and "daughter" has a room to herself but it really wasn't to herself. As I would call "daughter" she would never be available or she would not return my emails on the same day. "Mother" knew something was going on.

Deciding to take a break from whatever was going down there because "mother" did'nt know really what r or think and "daughter" was in another state. I deci take a break from my feelings and called a friend a praying woman who I admire as not only a p surely a praying woman who I call my big sister i We met for lunch just to talk and she says I sa now my friend is in the same state as I am a who was suppose to be in another state in sc wait hold up, she's her here. "Mother" was composure and not seem as fired up as sh inside bout to bust within the same we church says the same exact thing that

"Mother" knew she had not gon "daughter" did not have a car at so who knows what's going on? there after that the person fro "daughter",it had come out th and was seen by the the two i school thinking "mother" n and the phone call comes college is not for me thi long, of course there influenced this plan to get "daughter" f a call from "daug or heard of coul the young lad the approval

w
h
"
m
wa
the
she
wher
about
"daugh
did not
drove an
seat incog
over her h
anything .
gas and of c
parked "da
and friend.
about, helloo
talking as the
is no where in
wind literally I
about things all
restroom still in

the problem. Unbeknown to me the room mate is gone and "daughter" has a room to herself but it really wasn't to herself. As I would call "daughter" she would never be available or she would not return my emails on the same day. "Mother" knew something was going on.

Deciding to take a break from whatever was going on down there because "mother" did'nt know really what to do or think and "daughter" was in another state. I decided to take a break from my feelings and called a friend of mine a praying woman who I admire as not only a pastor but surely a praying woman who I call my big sister in the Lord. We met for lunch just to talk and she says I saw "daughter" now my friend is in the same state as I am and "daughter" who was suppose to be in another state in school, you mean, wait hold up, she's her here. "Mother" was trying to hold her composure and not seem as fired up as she really was on the inside bout to bust within the same week someone from the church says the same exact thing that had saw "daughter:

"Mother" knew she had not gone down to pick her up& "daughter" did not have a car at the time, "oh my God", so who knows what's going on? God surely did. Shortly, there after that the person from the church that had seen "daughter",it had come out that"daughter" had gotten a ride and was seen by the the two individuals and had gone back to school thinking "mother" never even knew. Well time went by and the phone call comes in "I' WANNA COME HOME", college is not for me this lasted every bit of 6 months if that long, of course there was a plan from another source that influenced this plan that was in the making. On the way to get "daughter" from school before leaving "mother" gets a call from "daughter" to ask if a friend she has never met or heard of could get a ride to Jersey. "Mother" speaks with the young lady mom to okay the ride back home and gets the approval all the long "mother" suspects something is not on the up and up. Upon arrival to the school "daughter" is packed and surely ready to go while "mothers" dream of her daughters College Graduation day goes down the drain. "Daughter" calls for her friend and everyone heads to the car while in "mothers" mind the wheels are turning saying I can't believe this after several, several trips on the weekends to the college for visits, pop ups or expected, things seemly to have working and going well, believing college life would help her get focused but yet she wasn't focused at all. Not on school at least and to top things off there would be another trip to get the remaining of her belongings. Also knowing weeks later there would be a return trip in a van to get the heavier belongings that were placed in storage was annoying "mother" along with not understand how did things go from wanting to be there to wanting to leave and come home . On the drive home "mother" talks with the friend about school, she was only coming home for the weekend, she talked about where she was from, what she likes to do, and a little bit about church, because all of "daughter" friends referred to "daughters" mother as is your mother a preacher or if they did not see "mother" where is your mother at church. As we drove and continued to talk "daughter" sits in the passenger seat incognito with a big grey hooded sweater with the hood over her head and her face toward the window barely saying anything . After driving for an hour or so its time to stop for gas and of course get something to eat before the car is barely parked "daughter" takes off and walks ahead of "mother" and friend. Well wow what in the whirl wind was that about, helloooo! "Mother" and friend continue walking and talking as they entered the restaurant to eat and "daughter" is no where in sight. Then suddenly as a rushing mighty wind literally I mean "daughter" was so quick and speedy about things all of a sudden. So "daughter" comes out of the restroom still incognito as "mother" says what would you like to eat "daughter" replies nothing, I have a stomache. "Mother" orders food and her and 'daughters" friend sits down to eat and continue to talk, "daughter" sits two seats away and puts her head on the table with the hood covering her head. This raised suspension more and more of what the heck is this about as "mother's" mind went into deep think mode and then I could hear my pastor saying as she has often said to me you think so much. However, curious George must have came in the invisible and tapped me on the shoulder because "mother" wanted to hurry up and get home to get "daughter" alone. Curiosity surely does not get you anywhere but "mother's" suspicions and suspense surely got her a speeding ticket out there driving tearing up that turnpike driving like that, switching them lanes and stuff, "mother" was wrong as two left shoes. After slowing down and trying to keep cool after the state trooper issue the ticket we arrive to NJ drop off friend "mother" says some things to the friend but really rushing her off thinking I hope the driving didn't wasn't to much for you. After pulling off we still can't get home quick enough as "mother" and 'daughter" both are in silence we get lost daa how you get lost in towns you know you are familiar with driving well maybe "mothers" lesson was slow down surely you don't want to get another ticket We arive to the house when all of a sudden, look and behold there is this "silver ball" shining in "daughters" mouth "mother" did not want to face the reality that in spite of numerous discussions of asking her NOT to pierce her tongue she did anyway. Well "mother" flew off the handle, what a tongue ring!!! I thought we discussed you would not get one, okay well since you went and did it anyway if you get an infection in your mouth don't come to me!!! Was the place sterile?!!! When?? Where did you get this from??? Where did you get the money from?!! Never mind I don't want to know. Surely after getting home "mother" and "daughter" cool down now it is time to talk what are you going to do now? Take a break, a break, a break from what? You did'nt do anything really and you weren't down there but a minute, "mother" needed the break, please!!! Okay, there were some struggles down there "daughter" said but I really don't want to get into it and I'm not doing anything, of course your not, I didn't say that you were, "mother" said. Now things are hot and they are heavy the hanging out started right away. I'm grown, I don't have to go to church EVERY Sunday and I'm not, and I'm not gonna make you know promises about church, I've been in church all my life. Oh yeah, okay, now I may not be able to make you go to church but you will go to work or school or how bout both. Oh, my goodness every other month was a new job and "daughter" barely went to work but she kept getting new jobs, my my my job after job after job you get and people that want to work can't even get a job. Then there was no job and no school at all, and the hanging out got worst and worst, the coming in got later and later, this had to stop. There was just no way that this was happening one confused thing behind another not wanting to abide by the rules or regulations of the house. Yes you may very well be grown or an adult but your sure not acting like one and if you were living with someone else in their house or on your own. How are you going to have food, clothing, and shelter without a job? You surely are not going to live disrespectfully and defiant in this house just because you are grown. Before things get any worst it was time to go deeper and dig deeper to try to come to an agreement or this is not going to work. ."Daughter" would say okay that she would be willing to try to do better in one breath and do another and lie in the next. It was like doctor jeckle and mr. hyde, an emotional roller coaster like some sort of chemical inbalance, or was it substance abuse. There were so many questions to all of this so out of "daughters" character where is this behavior that was going on coming from. Although all these things were happening in the natural "mother" knew that behind every natural situation there was spiritual action for and behind this that could bring a solution,"mother' just did not quite still have the certainty she was looking for. Then there was times where it seemed like "daughter" was acting bipolar because she would wanna be saved not be saved, pray not pray, receive the word, not receive the word. How could the child that I carried for 9 months and raised it seemed like I did not this person that was living the same roof and the things that would come out of her seemed like some other person was using her mouth. Her brain definitely seemed like it was fried or something but there seemed to be no signs of the drugs I wanted to find and blame this on. It was time to face some serious facts what was going on was soon to revealed and it wasn't good .

Phase 3
* I'm Moving Out *

This afternoon started out as what had become usual for "daughter" it was a typical day for her the typical day was she was like a moving target continually she was what I call all over the place never stable at this point she didn't know what she wanted to do and never staying still long enough to find out. She was not keeping a job and she decided she would start back pursuing her singing career going into the studio with a music teacher from High School. Singing for "daughter" started at the age of three, which at 3yrs of age "daughter" actually sounded like Coko from the group SWV, and she loved Shirley Caesar songs !!! Weeks prior was day in and day out going into the studio and it would turn into gone all day and all night. Once again "mother" felt this was not what was really going on although "daughter" was laying it on thick making it seem as if she was really enjoying her music and wanted it to really go somewhere and that would be what she would make as her career. Things were going well for "mother" excited about the things of God and the things he had been doing in her life and at church. The Lord had lead "mother" on a 3 day fast and prayer consecration with no food and no water. "Mother" had done this once or twice with the church but it was the first time doing it "alone". On the second day of this prayer and fast after getting home from work and really feeling weak in the body but her spirit was lifted. "Daughter" was aware of the fast and prayer and asked if she could pray for "mother" before she went to the studio on this day as she told 'mother" she was about to head out and would not be out long tonight. We prayed, we hugged and "daughter" was off to the studio. Well the enemy was in for the kill this night "daughter" broke the record she stayed out later than she had ever ever stayed out before. Troubled by this "mother" began to ring "daughter's" cell phone. "Daughter" answered and said she was still in the studio and would be home shortly. Well, what kind of studio is this a 24 hour studio? Another hour or two went by and another phone call to the cell phone followed by several calls but "daughter" would not pick up. By this time "mother" could not sleep and went into the bathroom one of my favorite spots for prayer and I was so weak from the fast I layed on the floor praying all of a sudden "mother" began to weep and ball up in a fetal position travailing in the spirit and speaking in an unknown language to myself. "For if I pray in an (unknown) tongue, my spirit prayeth, but my understanding is unfruitful". (I Corinthians 14:14 KJV). Then there was silence and quiet for a long while when from the bathroom "mother" could hear the door open. As "mother" arose and went to go to look at the clock that struck 4am and confront "daughter" there was a look on "daughters" face that "mother" had never seen this one before that if there was such an appearance of the devils face. "Mother" was facing him before her very weak eyes and weak body. "Daughter" was acting distraught and very agitated and before long words turned into an argument, an argument into a physical altercation, and before I knew it "mother" and "daughter" were in a brawl on the floor. There was screaming!!! And hollering!!! As "mother's" mother (grandma) came out of her room yelling, STOP IT!!! STOP IT!!!.. Trying to pull two generations apart her "daughter" and her "granddaughter" from satans attack . Yells and screams lead to cries and sobs as now three generations were in turmoil the brawl continued for minutes more with 3 tired bodies lying on the floor by the front door as "daughter" screamed outttt!!

Get off of me I'm leaving!!!. In the midst of all the commotion "daughter's" cell phone rings and she manages to answer it as one of us was laying on top of it while the 3 generations are on the floor still and she answers and says I'm coming now. The brawl comes to an end and everyone is out of breath and "daughter" begans packing a bag, "mother" is trying to stop her, and grandma is sitting blocking the door begging and pleading saying NOOOO!!!! I won't let you leave us. As the cell phone rang continuously "daughter" kept answering saying I'm trying to come, okay, I'm coming, after numerous attempts to plead for "daughter" to stay "daughter" began to get more and more hostile. "Mother" said to grandma "ma" let her go. "The plan worked". Downstairs waiting was someone in a car to get "daughter" away from her family and this was "the plan" all the long. I call it "the get away car" was waiting. Waiting to take away my "baby" from her family although she was 18yrs old and she wanted to go. "Daughter" crabbed her bag and was gone a broken hearted grandmother slid to the floor at the door as she crabbed her chest and she cried please!!! Don't go!!!. "Mother" went over to help her mother up off of the floor as they both cried together. After all hell had broke loose there came a silence over the whole apartment after all the commotion had died out that could have woke up all the neighbors in the building. You could hear a pin drop on the carpet it was so silent in between the soft cries of "mother" in one room, and a grandmother in another room. "The plan had worked ", the devils plan had worked, so he thought anyway, to separate a God fearing family. Well by this time it was 6am in the morning and "mother" had made it through her prayer and fast but by this time the devil began to knock at the door of "mother's" heart, and pick and poke fun at her brain with guilt, saying see!! What you just did and your suppose to be a christian and not only that you were fasting, that's a shame. Not only was the fast over but "mother" felt life her life was over as she picked up the phone and called a family friend who's like family as well as an evangelist who offered a scripture from the psalms("They that sow in tears shall reap in joy" psalm 126:5 KJV). Trying to find comfort in that scripture did not come that quick, that instantly. It all felt like I was hearing but not hearing. Later on that morning I called my pastor and we had prayer, after I showered and got dress I went to a sister in Christ church who has 6am prayer every morning Mon – Fri and I often went to these prayers before work, those sisters don't miss a day and they know how to pray and praise God. As I walked to the church because I did not have a car at the time and the church was only about 4 blocks away I felt like a walking mummy. I sat quietly the whole hour trying to hear from the Lord and trying to understand what just happened only two hours ago with puffy red eyes and not having been sleep since the day before oblivious to anything around me. "Mother" felt like Hannah, "Now Hannah, she spake in her heart; only her lips moved, but her voice was not heard: therefore Eli thought she had been drunken", I Samuel 1:13, KJV). Thank God for all the praying saints that he has put in my life and thank God those sisters in Christ have discerning of the spirits because they could of thought I was very well drunk or high one or the other or both. I surely probably looked out of it because still hadn't eat all the fast was over just surviving off water. I finally went back home called out from work and the rest of the day and night was

a total blur. The next morning in prayer kneeled at the side
of the bed before I walked to the church I quietly heard the
Lord say "This is only for a season". Thing is, spiritual seasons
are not like seasons in the natural.

So truly "mother" had no idea how long or how short the
season would be I couldn't even think of what was the shortest
season in the natural but yup I choose that one. Well it all
must have happened close to Sunday because Praise the
Lord!!! Halleulah !!! Sunday rolled around but to be honest
"mother" was not in her Sunday's best, mood that is if you
would if you looked at Sunday religiously or traditionally.
Now, no one at church really knew what had happened but
pastor and one of the church elders at the time but you know
how the devil does he works 24/7 so he was at work probably
at the church door like a parking garage attendant waiting
for me to show up, waiting also to make me feel like everybody
knows and their all watching you. Oh please it's not like that
devil, that would not be "mother's" case at her church. No
need to feel embarrassed or a total disgrace. My immediate
family and I touched and agreed, there is power in agreement,
we were gonna go to church with our heads and our spirits
lifted up nothing changes we have to pull it together and still
go praise God and we did just that "Lift up your heads, O ye
gates; and be ye lift up, ye everlasting doors; and the King of
glory shall come in" Psalm 24: 7 KJV). At church I had
spiritual amnesia because I did not remember the message
and my heart felt like it was in ICU spiritually in some type
of spiritual coma my body was in church but my mind was
on the other side of town trying to find a missing "daughter".
"Mother" could not place a missing person "daughter" was
18 and she was not missing she willing left home. My brain
waves were speeding with numerous thoughts of
condemnation ("So now there is no condemnation to those
who belong to Christ Jesus" Romans 8:1, NLT). and although

no one else heard the voices of hell, all I could hear was you failed as a "mother" it's all your fault. God is good all the time because the time had passed and "mother" and her family made it through church service but it felt like I was in church for weeks or months this was the only time ever in the 7yrs I had been at my church at that time and I was thinking when church gone be over. Days would past and my family and I did not know where my "daughter" was, where she had gone? One week went by and I felt like it was more like one year. This particular Sunday morning was better than the last "mother" was ready to go to the house of the Lord although still aching but there was a strange feeling that "mother" felt "daughter" would return while the family was in church but instead of staying home to see if what I felt was correct I felt more lead to still attend service. Service was uplifting and "mother" enjoyed it very much but I guess the spiritual amnesia would take a while to get over or was coming back or some thing because I was happy to hear God's word and how he used my pastor but I kept saying what did pastor say? That feeling about "daughter" was not strange after all because when the family returned home "daughter" had made a quick visit while we were in church and was gone again before we got back. "Mother" could tell she gathered more of her things but there was a bag that she left behind. It was actually a bag of "daughter's things she had brought home from college that she never unpacked but kept safely secured and privately stored in a closet. Well, as all parents often say nothing of their children's is private if it's in your house but she was grown but as the parent and you pay the rent and the bills, oh please and if there is a suspicion children you can hang it up. So after maybe I should, maybe I shouldn't and back and forth and so on. You, know how the saying goes, if you see something you don't want to see it is your own fault. Don't go looking for trouble you just might find it.

Well, "mother" is risky by nature so "Mother" began to look through the bag. There to "mother's" surprise she found a letter and pictures of the girl "daughter" was involved with. With tears and pain, feeling and think this can't be, staring at the picture for minutes again seemed like hours "mother" could not stop staring should I go off on the picture should I not be a Christian for a moment and tell her off through the picture. How many roller coaster rides could "mother" take in her mind of emotions because naturally I can't even ride one scared to and they make me dizzy and sick well that's about how I was feeling like I was on a roller coaster for years leading up to this day. Finally a face to match the voice that "mother" had been hearing for about 2 years prior but never understood what was going on, after all she was in college at the time and "daughter" was a innocent High School girl so mother thought and felt like this older young college girl had taken advantage of a young high school girl. When she had started calling "daughter" was 16 and the phone would ring at around 11pm every night with this voice on the other end asking for "daughter" at 1st "mother" thought nothing of it other than the hour was a little late and who was she why I didn't know who she was and had never met her and why she only calls at night. "Daughter" always had an excuse and always said "mother" is just always thinking something that's its not, well you always have an excuse and all excuses were nailed to the cross "mother" would tell "daughter". So one night the clock struck the 11th hour phone rings and "daughter" jumps to get the phone and as she's talking the Spirit of God speaks to "mother" and say that's an inappropriate conversation so "mother" immediately tells "daughter" exactly what the Spirit said the Holy Ghost just said that's an inappropriate conversation and "mother" says hang up the phone now. Now that this evidence and proof was all gathered "mother" felt like inspector gadget, Matlock and was ready to go to trial.

It was very hard for "mother" to be ye angry and sin and let not the sun go down on your wrath. I knew the scripture I knew to pray and fast but I was in tug a war because I wanted love this young girl but at the same time I wanted to fight. Let's be honest no one stays in the Spirit ALL the time the bible says the Spirit will not always strive with man but I had to find a way to wage a spiritual warfare with the weapons of God oh but this was difficult. I had to let love and prayer be for my "daughter" and the other young girl but I had to fight in the Spirit for my "daughter" who knew the way and because she was my "daughter" I was not sure of what the young girl back round was I did not know anything about her at all and honestly I wasn't really interested. I thought in my mind maybe once "daughter" was free then maybe I'll come back and get you. It was like the underground rail road I had to go free my "daughter" and then maybe down the line I will come back through and free some other young folk but I had to see my way through to free "daughter" out first. Like how can I do this I needed a stratergy and I didn't have one and I had to dig deep in the manual the bible to figure this out how do you go about this one. I knew no one else at the time that had really gone through it and had come out really most of all those that were in this lifestyle or love ones that had love ones in it was kind of "mothers" situation or those that felt that nothing was wrong with it, it was just how God made some people and that he still love them if I had to tell one more time what the bible said on it and yes he love them but not the sinner I was gone go buy my own trumpet and blow, blow, blow it the city of Newark and every city there of. So my plan was get "daughter" first and then okay God I will let you help me to help somebody else and let this young girl be last because I was angry with her and I had to keep asking God to help me be mad with the spirit that operated in her not mad at her. However, God ways are not our ways and his thoughts are not like our thoughts but higher and he has no respect of person so yeah I had my plan but God had his plan.

"Mother" was ready her first time ever to go to jail because if she ever saw this girl she was going to get the beating of her life. Not only that "mother" had a possible address because of course her address was on the letters that was in the packed away bag.

Oh my God Holy Ghost!!! Please restrain "mother" the hood is trying to come back, after all "mother" had grown up in the projects and fight was a must at some point and time. There was also this teddy bear with a necklace around it, this made "mother" more furious and as if that was not enough with the letter now a stuff animal come on stop it you gotta be kidding me, then "mother" finds this letter to the girls mother from "daughter" telling the girls mother how much she was the mother she always wanted. "Mother" had to stop looking at this point because this ripped my heart to shreds I felt like I was dying as if my heart was skipping beats and at that point that would have been fine by me. I was in so much pain and agony just by what I read now even to hear the enemy picking rubbing it in like wow can you believe what she wrote I knew "daughter" could never mean that after all we were very close as a family what would make her say such a thing. "Mother" tried to encourage her own heart you were not and you still are not perfect but you were and still are a good "mother" to her. A church mother once said to me: "When children are young they lay in your lap, when they are older they lay in your heart". This was so profound for me at that moment as it came back to my troubled heart for there were many nights my mother was picking me up off the floor shaking uncontrollably, while I would say Ma I can't take it ma!!!, I can't!!!, I would get stuck in the shower and just start screaming and my mother would come get me

31

out of the shower embracing me saying come on, you've got to make, we're gonna make it and I would cry and cry and say nooooo!!! I can't ma I can't, and she would say yes you can and you will. Waking up and going to sleep was something I just did not want to do anymore. My job was very busy and very demanding and getting there everyday was getting harder and harder. Day by day, morning, noon, and night the crying, the anxiety, the lack of sleep was taking a toll on my mind. I would cry where ever I went, in the house, in the street, in the store, in the car, I remember crying many times on the bathroom floor at work then wiping my face and going back to work. One day I sat down at my desk and I was trying to work and I had a memory lapse of what I was doing I could not for the life of me remember my job I did not know how to perform my duties. I would forget who was on hold and why. This would happen often until I broke out crying at the desk one day and one of the young ladies took me in a private room and began to pray for me. I was so out of it my cries would not let me hear the prayer. I continued to draw blanks at work and I could not remember what I was suppose to be doing with accounts, my car got repossessed, money was funny, and my physical body was just shutting down. I tried to get a leave of absence from my job which was not available at the time that it led me to resign from my job. This crying went on for months, maybe about 3 months, almost non stop like clock work. In my sleep out of my sleep it really was like a "Sleepless night in Seattle". I remember my nephew saying one night as I was crying walking through the house like an emotional wreck, while he was watching TV, auntie it's not a matter of IF she come home, it's WHEN. I walked away boo hooing, shaking my head like a little kid, like when daddy says to child its gone be okay baby, as I said okayyyy with my voice shaking. I wonder did my nephew say that because I was disturbing what he was watching on TV and he was like I wish she be quiet and trust God or was he really encouraging me, he was 9 at the time going on 19. "I forgot to ask him". "Mother" started trying to get some kind of grip on her emotions and the bible does say a child shall lead the way right. (smile). Then all of a sudden.

Phase 4
* Girls, Girls, Here, There, Girls, Girls, Everywhere *

Things are not over but there is a settling down. A song writer wrote I can see clearly now the rain is gone. The spiritual rain storm/hurricane had surely hit my area but my spiritual vision and perception was filled with some light, the sun was coming out, the storm had ceased and brought a calm and comfort. The burden was still heavy but there was a lifting. Lets go back Jesus began to say to my heart and brought back to my remembrance what I had read in John 14:26 KJV "But the Comforter, (which is), the Holy Ghost, whom the Father will send in my name, he shall teach you all things, and bring all things to your remembrance, whatsoever I have said unto you." As I was being taken back into some of the times of the past God reminded me of in "daughters" first year of High School she switched from an Catholic High School to a public school the 2nd semester that did not go well for "daughter" grades wise or association wise. However, "mother" could not afford the cost to pay for schooling anymore so a mother had to do what a mother's got to do. She had been attending catholic school all her life so "mother" knew this would be different for her, a challenge and it was.

Well that particular High School didn't work for "daughter" and she had to switch to another school which was known to be a rough school, in a rough area, again mother had to do what mother had to do. The weekend before she began the new school the Spirit of God spoke to my heart to go with two other praying saints to go to the school to pray around the building before "daughter" would start the school. All though we could not get legal access to pray inside the school we knew that God will allow our prayers outside be effective and impact inside the school God is just awesome like that. The three of us approached the school knowing a three fold cord is not easily broken and that Jesus was in the midst of our gathering because the bible said he would be. Again, we approached the building watchful as well as we walked onto the property prepared opening our mouths praying. (Shout out to those prayer warriors!!!). It was cold and dark for the sun had gone down early in this winter month and it was very cold bitter cold. As we walked I walked in the front with the two warriors behind me in prayer as I held my bible open to the Lord as I read his word in the atmosphere using the night lights that surrounded the school building declaring the 91st psalm and Ephesians 6 chapter wearing the whole armor of God. There were people that we passed at the bus stop right in front of the school looking at us as though we were strange we praised God and smiled, said God bless you and kept right on walking and praying. We did not even know at the time that the school had a night school program and people were in the school and we saw people go in and out and we continued on just the same.

The presence of God was with us and we knew that he was I felt this was the seal of God's protection over "daughter" going there. "Daughter" did not know that this had taken place although "daughter" knows that If God leads "mother" to do anything if it's God "daughter" knows 'mother" gone do it. She also know that "mother" will go to the extreme so she feels because she always told the story of when "mother" beat her as a teenager in the church usher room because she acted up in school and she just kept saying ma I was in High School dag, lol.. Well, shortly after "daughter" had began attending the school she began to come home and speak of how there was a strong spirit of homosexuality in the school and that was her wording. My family and I heard so many gross stories regarding this lifestyle IN THE SCHOOL it was unbelievable, I just believed for "daughters" covering from this spirit. 2 yrs later "daughter" graduates from this school but this spirit had already found a resting place in my "daughter's" heart and mind and began to eat away all that she had learned and been taught she had been brought up in the church and taught right at home so what in the world!.

This was totally against the order of God and our family morals and values. Again I must keep saying this God loves the homosexual and lesbian and so do I but he does say in the bible this is not his will he does not except it or approve of it he did not make you born this way. The other thing "mother" could not understand was that it was no one in her family on her mother side or father side that was in this lifestyle as 'mother" researched both sides of the family. The standard of our home was being violated big time. I had to stay determinded, keep the faith, and not give up. "Not without my daughter" devil no, no way I don't have to except nothing that's not in the word of God how about that, how you like them apples. I had to learn how to pray for my "daughter's" deliverance and at the same time love those who were in this lifestyle those that were not saved and that were saved but in it, hiding it, struggling with it whatever the case, heaven only knows, but it was serious yall. This was the HARDEST thing in MY LIFE (thus far) that I ever had to deal with and face. We may not want to deal with and face our child or children's problems because they are so painful, but with no other choice I mean I had no other choice if I was gone live right as best as I knew how so was I going without my 'daughter". I mean like the movie that the title of this book was inspired by the Holy Spirit in my heart in short if the "mother"(Sally Fields) in the movie was gone escape death she was not gone leave her "daughter" behind she was escaping with her 'daughter". It's like getting saved and going to heaven and your salvation is secure but you not gone get insurance to cover your child or children also just a way to put it to get the point across. No, sometimes parents/or a parent may not want to deal with face our child or children's problems when they are especially grown but they are still ours and we do have a responsibility to pray for them and tell them the truth. I began in prayer to feel the burdens for other "daughters" not just my "daughter" in the lesbian lifestyle. It could be a sister, niece, aunt, cousin, friend, daughter, whoever she just needed to be of course female and that was the hard because there was a lot of females so many coming across my path feeling or thinking they are and were born male or wanted to play the male part. This was not something I wanted to take on, or could take on my own. I did not want to hear, think, or see it. It was like the movie hear no evil, see no evil I just did not want any part of it I guess prior to "daughter" I never had to deal or think of it much and sure seemed like they were all in hiding but then it was like the earth was just invaded or something it was like every which I went with no exaggeration there she was and she was into the lifestyle and "mother: did not know whether to get angry or whether to cry." God had a plan". God speaks again and sends me back to the school this time with the instruction to pray against the spirit of homosexuality/lesbianism over that school. Of course I am like what God? You know I don't like that spirit, and my "daughter" don't even go there anymore and the damage is already done. I was upset with God and this made me angry because I could not understand this whole thing anyway and then I could not realize at the time this was a spiritual thing not a natural thing. I sort of kind of knew but I was stuck like what God? You want me to do what? Go where? Out of wanting to obey God and get pass being angry with God because I love him so much I went to my pastor to tell her and she began to counsel me and give me instruction and of course pray for me. She shared with me how God would have her do similar things for his glory to show others there is a God and that prayer absolutely changes people, places and things. Prayer can go and do what no man can do and where no man can go, above and beyond. I got 3 other saints this time and the 4 of us went on the assignment. We covered that school in prayer, we cried out to the Lord on the steps of the school in public in broad daylight, we cried out to God for the souls of those children to be saved, delivered, and set free that yokes would be broken and just utterly destroyed, and that the strong holds in their little minds would be pulled down and the imaginations would be cast out of their minds and covered in Jesus blood!!! All this while "daughter" was still in it doing her so called thing, so she thought and guess what so did I. We may not have the record of by number what happened but I heard a prophet of God say shortly after we were commissioned to that school, that we may not be able to openly pray in the school but thank God, we have prayer for the school in our hearts. So I know God did something there. After this, a series of events began to take place. Everywhere I went looked and turned I was surrounded with girls into that lifestyle still even the MORE it was girls girls, here there, girls girls everywhere. I thought, Oh my God this is disgusting, this is ill, I don't want to see this, I wanna close my eyes literally and act like I don't see it or so I don't see it, that didn't work because when I closed my eyes I would see visions when I slept at night there they were in my dreams I thought this is torment. I don't want to be around this, and then there would be some young girls that were so nice and respectful in this lifestyle and my heart would melt, then some were nasty, rude and disrespect and I would cringe and get angry this was just to much. I don't even want to hear it, it was like some of their conversations were so vulgar and disgusting it was the fact that two young girls were talking to each other like that OMG, then the fact that they were so young and "mother" couldn't understand or get how does someone so young talk all that and know all that stuff "mother" was like do they realize I'm sitting right here and I am an adult. It would ring in my ears long after I was gone from them lingering in my ears annoying my ears like water in your ears after going swimming and you hear the water moving around in your ears but it won't come out so you shake your head putting your ears to your shoulders and your shoulders to your ears like "come out" this is so annoying. It was on the news, tv shows, radio, when I was walking, driving, in the stores, again conversations I heard, elementary, high school, and college students and oh my God in the church!!! Then I would hear laughter and jokes about it and some of the laughter and jokes came from church folk and from preachers (some not all).

That was making me angry and course I took it personal when I heard a preacher joking about it when we know those that are bible readers that the bible says that you can go to hell for living in this lifestyle if you not repent and turn away from it. So you mean to tell me you think this is something to joke about preacher I see nothing funny about it and you know many people are into it and my child is. I was glad when I started hearing preaching against it but love for the individual because I was starting to feel like I was being tormented by all of this then the dreams and the perverse visions morning, noon, and night this was happening a lot that I was seeing this. I began to feel like Lord, what did I do wrong? Why is this my "daughter" going through this and she knew, I knew, we both knew? what did my family do wrong? Then God began to touch and soften my heart with love, compassion and revelation. The devil wanted to make me question God and he was trying to get me to hate the persons hate was trying to creep in but God would turn me to the answer of love and compassion for the girl who is in a lifestyle of lesbianism. The word has even gotten easier to say to pray over through the touch of God on my heart as well to pray against it and pray it off a these girls because I didn't even wanna say that name. The thing was, I could not believe what my "daughter" was out there involved in, it was God putting it before me not satan to intercede and pray on behalf of but satan was trying to make it so monsterous. What I wanted nothing to do with God began to give me not only a heart for but opportunities to witness on the street, he would send me by the school house, youth events, the doctors office, the store, at church where ever there was an opportunity God would graciously PLACE ME THERE. I would have dream after dream then I would come in contact with someone's "daughter" all the long my "daughter" was still in it and rebelling against 'mother" and the family did not except it but loved her. This was so difficult for me of course but I could not deny the tug of the Holy Spirit and the spirit of prayer over my life. My heart wanted to do what God wanted me to do but my mind kept telling me NO, you don't want this, but my heart kept saying YES. One day a pastor friend of mine called me and said you know God wants you to pray for these daughters your "daughter" are involved with the one she is personally involved with and the ones she hang out with or around. She went on to say you may even have to be around some of them and let your light shine. I thought yeah, yeah, I know but I really did not want that charge or call. Then a cousin of mine said to me one Sunday after seeing me at the altar praying with a "daughter" that God and delivered from this lifestyle. My cousin said to me I saw you in a vision praying for many "daughters" and God is going to free your "daughter" as he use you to focus on other "daughters" that you are encountering now to get free he's working on your "daughter" in the mean time. This ignited a fuel, a fire in my soul!!! Because it was like God had spoken twice, I have spoken once and twice had I believed that power belongs to God it was like out of the mouth of two or three witness's let every word be established this was bible that always gets 'mother's" attention you gone give me bible okay I see what I'm working with now. At that moment I began to hear God say that this is why you must go through this not stay in this but go through this, you gotta go through your go through in other words. Yea though I would walk through the valley of the shadow of death the Lord would be with me it was not just about 'daughter" the other daughter but it was about me too, what God was using me for to bring him glory. Why must I go through this? I never asked God that again, after that day, I GOT IT LORD!!! I thank him for using my pastor friend and my cousin at that point and I thank them for letting the Lord speak through them. Yes girls girls here there and every where were still coming and I was some time just simply talking with them not beating them over their heads with the bible and preaching to them how I did 'daughter' in the past because I would beat her with the word and everything was a preach that 'daughter' would say to me can you talk to me without preaching like you got a mic behind a pulpit we just talking. One day we were driving 'mother" was picking "daughter" up from school or work which ever one she was doing at that time and "mother" was angry because "daughter" seemed like she still wasn't getting it so "mother" starting going in soon as "daughter" got in the car. We were driving around down South Orange Ave leaving Livingston in NJ and anyone that knows that area know going around those curves and swirls can be something and "mother" was speeding around them speaking in tongues and "daughter" didn't know whether to be scared for safety of no accident or the power of the tongues telling the devil to go out the car and out of 'daughter". It was a summer day so the windows were down but "daughter" knew that "mother" didn't even care about as we stopped at the red light two men were in a truck beside them and the two men heard "mother" speaking in tongues and they were smiling saying praise him sister yes praise him while "daughter" was probably thinking she done lost her mind I

aint even say nothing and she all going off in tongues I don't even know what she talking bout. As we arrived home "daughter" got out the car so fast before the car fully stopped "daughter" was walking so fast like a walking marathon saying you crazy and all "mother" could say was more tongues I can't even type them because I don't even know what the spirit was saying myself. Yet "mother" did not use that approach with the girls she would just pray and give them the scriptures. Yes, the very thing that took my "daughter" away from her home, her family, was the very thing, the very area, God began to use "mother" in, constantly, and it was bringing some "daughter's" out but not mine, patience was a virtue that I had to learn. I had to remember to stay FOCUSED and believe what God did for others he would do for me that if I took care of God's business he would be sure mine get done and it would be by him that it would get done. When God is always stirring up something to show he's getting ready to come through and deliver the devil will get schizophrenic and don't know what to do but keep stirring up the prayers keep stirring up the tongues God is about to show up.

"God Is Still Using the Youth"

With God nothing is impossible. Although "daughter" had left home I always had a heart for the youth so anytime there was a prayer gathering or an event for the youth I was sure to attend whether 'daughter" was with me or not. There was a particular Youth Summit Event that I attend at another church in support of our church youth. As I sat in the background in the midst of this anointed service I began to pray fervently for the youth at this church and the youth at my church. Although "daughter" was on my mind something happened there that touched my heart that I will never ever forget. God through the Holy Spirit took me out of my thoughts for "daughter" and brought me into a spiritual encounter with his Spirit connecting my heart with the hearts of the youth that were present in the service. I saw with my very own eyes in an instant God change the heart and mind of somebody's daughter, she had to be around the same age as my "daughter" at the time, about 18 yrs old. The praise and worship had gone forth in power with the youth yielding themselves to God, the youth preacher had preached the word of God with the anointing, power, and conviction. God's word, the awesome worship, and the praises coming out of the mouths of the youth had the atmosphere of the sanctuary soaked with the tears of the youth crying out. Giving their hearts to God, gifts were being demonstrated, signs and wonders followed "It was an awesome sight to see". To see God's glory like that especially on "teenagers" this is one of my biggest joys to witness. God's glory on "teenagers" wowww!!!! So back to the what happened when I saw God change this young lady life. In the midst of all this glorious wonder God allowed me to see satan at work in the sanctuary(the nerve of him, satan in God's house). However, thanks be to God, what the devil meant for evil

God will work it out for our children's good because of the POWER, in INTERCESSORY PRAYER. THE BIBLE, says the effectual fervent prayer of a righteous man availeth much. Check that out in James 5:16 halleulah!!! As these young people were receiving from God and the preacher was preaching with the fire of God on him I was seated directly behind this young lady who was hugging the two young ladies on each side of her as she went from side to side trying to indulge them in conversation this seemed to be the only section in the entire sanctuary under distraction and it had to be the row in front of me on the side I was on. Although that's what it looked like in the natural, the Spirit of the Lord showed me in the Spirit that, that spirit, was not the young lady, but, the spirit of satan (spirit of homosexuality), working through this young lady pimping these two young ladies to distract, to attract and attack. A young Spirit filled young lady in my church use to tease me saying you don't have radar you have gaydar not to pick or make fun of anyone but I knew she meant in the sense to detect to pray. As the Lord allowed me to see this young lady countenance and her motive, which was not really her at all but the countenance and motive of the evil one satan. The Lord touched my heart to not get mad at her or annoyed with her but mad with the devil for trying ti disrupt the service and that he wanted me through his power to make satan shut up hold his peace and come out of that beautiful young lady someone 'daughter" he was trying to hold hostage by lying to her. He allowed me to see beyond and to see that there was a need for me to begin praying for her. As I bowed my head the Holy Spirit prayed through me for this young lady, the preacher was making the altar call at the same time for the young people, and at the same time saying parents get with your children and if your child is not hear pray for someone else's child as if your child was here or as if you would want someone to pray for your child with that child you get with.

As I lifted my head to my surprise, it was for me like a surprise birthday party that I never had, but when you walk into the house or place everybody yell surprise!!! And you see all these people, family, friends, love ones, maybe people you have not seen in a longgggggg time maybe even years, and your so excited and happy word can't express you just gasp and grab your face with a joyful heart, tears of happiness and emotions stir and you just look around with so much happiness. This is how I felt when I opened my eyes and saw the alter flooded with the youth crying out, shouting, praising, worshipping, speaking in tongues (their heavenly language unto God), the pulpit was so large in that church it was like a stage the stage where the preacher was, and the other men and women of God were also so full of joy as the youth were receiving an anointing from God as the preacher was praying and laying hands on them they were receiving the Holy Ghost on the stage some of them the preacher hands never reached them they were falling walking up the steps falling on top of each other on the stage by the power of God's spirit on them. The pews were filled with young people, using their gifts flowing, some you could tell that it was they are minister and operate in their gifts, some you could tell it was their 1st time but boldness was all in the building through the dynamite power of God Almighty. They were praying for one another, laying hands on one another, the place was packed with God's presence and no one was just sitting either it was standing room only or laying out on the floor. There was hardly a dry eye in the building, but tears were streaming down their young faces as there was so much shouting and dancing, there was surely no party like a Holy Ghost party, there were even some screams that you could hear in the spirit that said God's setting him or her free like God came down from heaven and went into hell and snatched the keys from the devil and loosed these children. It was a sight to see it was amazing, the two young ladies that was sitting on each side of the young lady the Lord had me praying for had left her side as the Spirit of God drew them to the altar and she was left alone. Others that she had also early on tried to distract was on their hands and knees, some laying prostrate, in front of her and in her row. I turned around to the back of me and to the side of me to see the wonder of God on these young people and when I turned back around in an instant the Spirit of the Lord had touched her heart and she the young lady herself was on her knees like a balled up baby as she began to yield and surrender and open her mouth in praise to God with her arms outstretched wide like she was about to fly a plane and take off Oh my God it was the most amazing thing I had ever encountered I knew my life from that for me and them, would NEVER be the same until I leave this earth I will NEVER forget that night it was like a dream come true. The Spirit of God so sweetly overshadowed her as she lay out on the floor calling on the name of Jesus!!! Just to hear her calling Jesus there is just something about that name that nothing else can compare. At that point when anybody calls on the name of Jesus!!! We know what that does, you shall be saved when you call on that name, I don't care who you are, girl, boy, man, woman, black or white, saved or not saved, if saved it's like a get saved some more ☺ God lost me for a minute as an intercessor. I lost myself in all this majesty as a matter of fact God did not need me then because she was calling him for herself so I could just bask in his presence with her. God was healing her as she was glued to that floor and could not get up until he was done. At the end of the service God whispered in my ear a word for her and told me to speak to her for she was someone else's daughter, love your neighbor as thyself, but when I looked again she was gone. As I gathered my things, hair and clothes sweated out (I had just had gotten my hair done just to have to get it done again ☺.)like how I use to do back in the day at party's I use to attend the last to arrive and the last to leave. The good thing about leaving this Holy Ghost party was that the high was a supernatural high and it would last in my spirit and I would not have a hang over, boy oh boy did I enjoy hanging out with the youth that night I was in my own little world and I was so happy to be a part and the young always like to have me on board because I was gone pray and give the word and be hard but I was also gone make them laugh with the sense of humor comical side God has given me and we gone laugh but we also gone be serious. So the young people would always tell "daughter" ya mom is cool and yall look like sisters instead of "mother" and "daughter" . So I fitted right in with them with my sweat suit and sneakers on just like them. What a fireball night!

As I reached the door to my surprise my hand and her hand there she was the young lady reached for the door at the same time as she told me to go first. As I looked at her she looked like I felt like she had, had a good time with this big smile on her face and looking like a different person her countenance was totally changed. I asked her if I could speak with her for a minute, she said yes, I spoke to her what God spoke to me regarding her, and she gladly received God said and they would receive his word with gladness. We embraced each other in God's love as if we had already known each other and then departed. Although I never saw this young lady again and don't remember her name, I'll never forget her and I believe God freed her and she never looked or went back.. Every daughter is somebody's daughter. I had to stay determined, keep the faith, not give up hope, "NOT WITHOUT MY DAUGHTER" Although after that night on the way home on the church van what had took place that night had to end in the natural and "daughter" was not out and not home my hope rested in the fact that "God is still using the youth" and with God nothing is impossible, IF, you believe. On the way home the church van was rocking and we all didn't want the night to end and we knew it was gone be on at church in the morning, it was Youth Sunday too. For real the youth had the fire still in their belly and they took it to another level that morning. The youth at our church started flowing harder and more coming out of them in their gifts. The fire kept spreading and the youth that didn't make last night out got the residue on that Sunday morning. It was like a good cooked meal and you wake up for those left overs. "Mother" was running around the auditorium like a loose cannon doing gym laps like she was in training for a track meet or something. At the time we were having service in a school auditorium. "Mother" would always take off running, shouting, dancing, and the family would lol at me. One Sunday if it was not that Sunday, it must have been a youth Sunday though because I remember having on sweats again with my hair in a ponytail like I was youth just liked to dress down have fun with them and run the devil out of town. I remember the fire of God came on me like a consuming fire I started my laps now the auditorium had a slope hill type of thing going on with an entrance and an exit and "mother" is not getting younger but "mother" was taking them laps up and down all around, in and out and the family was saying when is she gone stop, when is she gone get tired and it was like they said you were running with your arms up, but every time I got in the front where pastor and 1st man were my arms would go out and hit 1stman and his body would jump and jolt like a wind went by or through him. "Daughter" was not there to witness that but God was using "mother" to run for "daughter" to break through for "daughter" and the arms lifted was the win and the victory

that was to come!!!!Halleulah praise God! It was time to take
the win and know it's a win secured, I was on the home front
with the Lord I was surely on the winning team because if
God be for us who can be against us and greater is he that is
in us then he that is in the world. We have a winning streak
with the Lord our track record with him will always produce
a win and victory we can never lose with him. We are not
only conquerors but we are more than conquerors through
him that loved us. It was like a training keep praising, keep
praying, keep lifting him up and the diet was actually fasting
because some things only come out by prayer and fasting. So
although fasting is the food without body and sometimes
without water the inner man the spirit is being build and
renewed day by day. This was the regimen of the Lord it was
a strict discipline it took consistency and it was hard work
it was not easy to the flesh. However, "mother" knew that
they that come to God must believe that he is, and that he
is a rewarder to them that diligently seek him. There would
be a reward after all this and that, that not only "daughter"
would come out but many others would also. So the fire
would continue to spread through what God had ignited in
the youth but like how a fire man comes to put out a fire in
the natural to save lives the devil would try to quench the fire
in our young people because it would in the spirit it would
keep them alive or fire for God because god wants us to be on
fire for him because if we are luke warm he will spew us out.
The devil already knows his destiny which is a lake of fire that
burneth with brimstone, this is the fire God has prepared
for satan and the fallen angels and other as well will go there
but I don't have time to go there to explain that's not for this
book, but God does not want no one there but satan does he
wants company. We will refuse to join him!

Phase 5
* I'm Back *

"A family determined to move forward" We often hear the saying "the family that prays together stays together", it may not be said or quoted like that in the bible per say but it is true, and it is so many scriptures in the bible to support that families must pray and serve God. Joshua said in the book of Joshua "as for me and my house we will serve the Lord". Read Joshua 2:15. What an awesome Godly principle, families must pray together, serve together. We determined as a family that no matter what the matter my family was going to pray and not only pray but keep praying. "Pray without ceasing", (KJV I Thessolians 5:17). Jesus told us that we should always pray "And he spake a parable unto them, to this end, that men ought always to pray, and not faint",(KJV Luke 18:1). "Mother" would run into people on the street, get phone calls, and they all were saying the same thing they would say they saw "daughter" and how she was always asking them for money, wearing PJ's in the street, loosing weight, her hair was falling out, and as the young people say "looking a hot mess". At this time my family and I knew where she was living but we determined to not go after her, we trying our best to interfere with God. In the beginning "mothers" Dad tried on his own when we found out the address to where she was living, I pleaded with Dad not to, but as a grandfather he felt he had to try. Dad came back without "daughter" and described a very ugly scene. He said that "daughter" his granddaughter yelled, shouted, and screamed and defiantly told him no she would not return home and that if he touched her she would call the cops on him, no one was going to run or rule her life, she was an adult and I choose to live this lifestyle and no one will change it as she continued to yell don't touch me I mean it papa! Well, after still much pleading with "daughter" my dad could not convince her to come home, so in tears he walked away, shaking his head in disbelief and hurt from his little granddaughter who he took everywhere, and did everything with, they were always hanging out together, he is her papa. I never had saw tears from my Dad eyes in all the years of my life and 'mother" is in her thirties ish at this time but from my sister and my mom I heard of how my Dad cried I'm glad I did'nt see it. I have never seen my dad ever cry, he's always just been my hero, I've always been daddy's baby girl so to see him cry would be very emotional for me I would not be able to handle that at all, no way. Dad felt at that moment we lost her she's gone she to far in it, its nothing we can do to help her she don't even want our help she said his heart was heart more than anything that's all.

"Good days and Bad Days" that's how it was going, that's just the way it is. Yes indeed, when you DON'T live for God you will have good and bad, when you DO live for God you will have good and bad the better is this, when you live for God your Good days will out weigh your bad days that is not just a song that's true, so choose to live for God, it will be a good thing, you know why? Because if your day isn't good, guess what? He is good God is good even on a bad day. " O Taste and see that the LORD is good: blessed is the man that trusteth in him.(KJV). There were days when I had to embrace and pray with my Mom and she the same with me. One day as one of my sisters and I were trying to hang out together to have some fun and relieve our minds for a change. I was driving when suddenly behind the wheel I began to break down in a panic/anxiety attack. My sister helped guide the car over to park and she began to pray as the Lord help us get through that crazy bout from satan. That same day we tried to keep going to enjoy our day we were on our way to pick up my Goddaughter to have fun with her and she was funny. My family has this thing where one of our family fun past times is to get the little ones because children are funny, and they keep you laughing and bring joy to your life and to your heart.

So as we got it back together in the car when we get to my Goddaughter's house who happens to be very funny who keeps the family laughing, with singing, acting, and some of everything else, and happens to be an intercessor who will lay and pray prostrate at the age of 2yrs old, surely we could get some laughter going on through her today. Before 'mother" could make it across the street my sister is in the passenger seat literally doing flips in the seat hysterically crying "I want my niece back" I entered back into the car and my sister cried lets go bust that house door down and get her and bring her home. For a minute "mother" thought this bust would be good, lets go break her out, like two gansters on a mission from a movie or something. No, just kidding but we needed to pull ourselves together remain prayerful, calm, and determined to trust God because back in the day we might have done just that we did do stuff like that again but we had to remember our weapons are in prayer not natural weapons. A bad day but it worked out for the good. By this time "mother" was so overwhelmed I had resigned from my job because there were so many other things happening all around one behind another that it was just overwhelming, one of my sisters was in school taking some classes and she stop school and put her classes on her hold. We were getting weak and needed strength. I had people say to me like it was nothing no big matter there are so many people in that life style and they never come out even other Christians said this to me. I said "not my daughter" and I said it with attitude. I even had church folk and I quote that's a hard thing to come out of "not my daughter", I thought in my mind as I listened to them say I've had family members that's been in that for years "not my daughter". I've had a family member die in that lifestyle, "not my daughter", that is one of the strongest spirits to break, "not my daughter", it's in the schools, in many families, even in the church, "not my daughter". It was like I had to quit my job to pray for my 'daughter" full time because of all that was being said I felt alone besides my immediate family and few others that I said it was like it more so be said directly or indirectly to just let it go and it wasn't like let it go and let God I know, I saw and I heard the difference. It was just a I don't feel like fighting that spirit or I don't know how or both, look, this will be my full time job then and when she get free I will go back to the work in the world but right now this is my work this is my job and that's how I felt, with no pay coming in losing things, not able to have or buy things for a minute okay. What have you lost your mind what are talking or thinking about I could hear people think or say if they said it to me or not. The good days have got to come, we will make it, as a family. I remember before a good day even came I remember the devil was trying to pull "mother" into such a depression and that spirit knew my past because I suffered from depression at one point in my life for 11 yrs, well the devil also knows that God has brought me OUT so he really does not want a fight from me either because I will not just let that spirit come back and enter my life again without a fight. I mean that, the greater one lives on the inside of me now, although it tries. The bible says: And they overcame him (the devil) by the blood of the lamb and by the word of their testimony and they loved not their lives unto the death. Revelations 12:11. Ha ha ha devil this is a powerful truth . Having a testimony alone is a miracle it is a great day of victory to escape the clutches of the enemies grip, Let the redeemed say so whom he have delivered from the hands of the enemy 'what a day"!.

Every day after that I would take my nephew to school and we would pray all the way to school and all the way back home when I would pick him up and continue in the house everyday was our pattern. I began to gain strength and hope. I began to praise, worship, pray and read the word more and more. "Devil it's on" We as a family began to crab a hold of faith although "daughter" was still not home yet. We were determined a fire of God and for God was burning. We packed our hearts with prayers to fill the void, we prayed morning, noon, and night. I prayed in my sleep, my spirit was like an electronic alarm clock that would go off hour on the hour. I would jump up out of my sleep and pray and praise God for my "daughter".

"Things that go bump in the night"

I would be bumping into walls, instead of sleep walking I would be sleep praying. By any means necessary I would do whatever it took. I knew that there was a call of God on her life and I was not going to just let that go or give up on her. God invested a lot in her, her gifts, her anointing he had used her at a young age and I was going to stand in the gap for her. We were going to make it as a family, a team in unity, in agreement, we talked and said the same things and stuck to it. I could imagine the was trying to find another scheme. One day I was speaking on the phone with an evangelist friend of mine and she said that because of the call of God on "daughters" life I hope she knows that she's going to bring the judgment of God on that house that she's living in by her staying there. Very shortly after that I went by my mom's house one day as I daily do and as I knocked on the door to my surprise "daughter" opened the door and fell in my arms crying mommy, mommy. She had gotten put out of the house she was staying at saying "I'm Back" home. Well we enjoyed these days we were all like yessss, yeahhhhhh, she's back, she's home, what a relief. We enjoyed some talks just "mother" and "daughter" talk, we hung out together some, we had some food, fun, and laughter, did girly things etc, we hugged, we cried, we joked, we hiked and did our family usual "daughter" even came to church sometime. Then suddenly there was a "blast" from the past she was back but not really back. "Daughter" would began sneaking again and then when confronted she would openly confess her doings, this time it was worst because she would always laugh when she was confronted. What would make "mother" cry would make "daughter" utterly laugh, that was one of the most hurtful feelings a human being could emotionally feel. She began to laugh in my face with lying, disrespect, defiance etc, All sorts of manifestations began to surface that she had been doing while she was out there having her world of fun she thought, drunkenness, smoking, lesbian parties, tattoos everywhere, body piercings and only God knows what else. "For all that is in the world, the lust of the flesh, and the lust of the eyes, and the pride of life, is not of the Father, but is of the world."(KJV I John 2:16). I wanted my "daughter" back but not with all of this it became so sickening and disgusting, spending nights and weekends out I thought oh my God do I even want her living back home coming in with all of this stuff and I surely was not gone deal with the rudeless. One night I had a dream I was in a club and all this chaos and lewdness surrounded me as I saw "daughter" in a vision. I fought to break my sleep by calling on the name of Jesus and the blood of Jesus as I awakened. I fell to my knees in prayer for a while and I saw "daughter" again in a vision from head to toe as the spirit of God began to tell me she would be coming to the house.

I began to walk the floor in prayer this was around 3 or 4 in the morning and I felt an evil presence in the house. I began to rebuke the presence and then eventually fell back off to sleep on my knees as I often did and as the presence left when I heard, very quietly ma, ma and I heard the chain on the door shake. I thought I was dreaming as I realized "daughter" had decided to come home although it was around 6 or 7am by this time. As I looked through the peep hole "daughter" was dressed exactly how "mother" saw her in the vision. "Daughter" staggered in with the reeking smell of alcohol and her head tied in a head scarf. So many nights and mornings went on like this not knowing if she would show up or not, sometimes she would, sometimes she wouldn't, not knowing who she was with or where she was. "Mother" was so worn out I was getting times and days mixed up. It was time to have another heart to heart talk with "daughter" but it seemed as if "daughter's" heart was numb, okay let's get it straight you must go to school or work or how about both if your going to stay here. This behavior will not be excepted or tolerated here you know that. She chose to enroll in business school and then eventually work as well. Things seemed good for a couple of months but the partying continued but not as much. Then seemed to be a shift a change but it was still drama from one extreme to the next now "daughter" has a whole new group of acquaintances oh yeah she often did this she switched what she called friends every other month or so. With the new acquaintances came a new hang out called the "garage" which was one of her acquaintances parents "garage" behind there house. Back in the day when "mother" was hanging out there was actually a club called the "garage". One day "daughter" comes home "I like this boy" the next week I like this boy, and so on she played this role. Of course our family never met these acquaintances unless we asked. Finally one day we get to see this supposedly young boy that she liked and liked her and that went every bit of a couple of weeks, late nights coming from hanging at the "garage" "mother" would have to call her cell phone to find out what time she planned on coming home. Although this was not what "mother" wanted for "daughter" either it was better than hanging out with or being involved in that lifestyle "mother" felt. However the late nights were always followed by long showers "mother" thinking like what are you washing off, eating, and going straight to sleep or always talking on her cell phone until "mother" felt like all this was a set pattern that became very suspicious to "mother" I felt something new was going on was the old tricks and schemes going on. Then suddenly she was no longer interested in the boy at the "garage" She was liking some boy she had a crush on in High School but still hanging at the "garage" and hanging with the boy from High School it was like she was playing a game. Eventually she dropped out of school again but never told "mother" the school called the house that's how "mother" found out but she kept the job. Of course when confronted she made some excuse and said she was going to go back. "Mother" knew something was going on strange but I could not quite figure it out but of course as all "mothers" know. You know that you know when it is something up with your child or children you just have this deep down gut feeling, that something is up and if you really know your child or children especially in the Holy Ghost he will let you know and then naturally mother's just know I guess it's a mother thing. Was "mother" in for another I was not ready for this type of situation but I figured it was something or actually I knew that's what it was.

Phase 6
* Its' Not a Toy It's Nonnie's Boy *

Well isn't every mother's hope and dream that her child or children do better and make better decisions for themselves than she did? Isn't it true that mothers want the BEST of the BEST for their child or children? If your like me and made wrong choices doing wrong things like we all do so you don't want that repeated in or through your child. I always felt out of 4 children I was the worst of my mothers children, after all I was the baby so why not? Most of my family always said I was spoiled and had to have my way and as I got older, yeah I partied, hung out all the time, got drunk and didn't know when to stop. Hanging out back then for me was Tuesday through Saturday and even on Sunday at times a lot of times, I hung out with who ever was hanging so if that meant different people to hang out with to cover the week I did, although basically everybody I hung out with knew each other. So being that I had different people to hang out with, different people liked to hang out different places I had my favorite but I liked them all. I probably hung out in almost every bar in my city. It's a shame when you drink so much beer that the bartender call you that as a nickname, and oh as if that was not enough, drinking shots of Hennessy in single and double shot glasses with the men in the bar chasing it down with beer, banging on the counter when done waiting for the next shot. Monday night was the only night the bar got a break from having a seat for me, or the dance floor having a partner or even if I danced on it by myself. Drag racing, fighting or escaping fightings, shootings, stepping over trampled bodys on the floor especially in NY. My mother often said I was a tough piece of letter well put together back in the day with a temper that was like a blast!!!! Maybe "daughters" behavior is some your fault of course because of what you use to do but she had some of her own stuff for sure that I never did for sure like this right here. So yeah "mother" track record was no bed of roses. So in my mind guilty as charged kept ringing in my ears, that guilt was eating away at "mother" while the devil kept pressing rewind, with you deserve to get back after all you did. As time went by I thought Lord can you ever forgive me of all that!!!!!!!! And more, and the answer is yes, yes he can. Yes he did. "As far as the east is from the west, so far hath he removed our transgressions from us" Psalm 103:12 (KJV), transgressions with an "s" because God knew that there would be more than one single thing but that there would be many things that we would need to be given for not only is God a God of a second chance but many chances. I am greatful for the forgiveness. I knew God had forgiven me but this took years then I had to forgive my own self and even ask "daughter" to forgive me. Wow forgiveness is a powerful thing to forgive and to be forgiven brings so much healing, peace and joy. We all have dreams, big or small but what happens when that dream or dreams that you have are being shattered right before your eyes. Dreams "mother" and the family had for "daughter" were being shattered even dreams "daughter" had talked of, of her own were being shattered behind being in this lifestyle it was just confusing every and all things nothing good was coming out of it nothing. If this was a game when was the game going to be over and this was a dangerous game who wants to play this time of game and it wasn't even fun.

You know one of those days where the family sit at the table to talk, have a seat make surrrrrrre your sitting down and comfortable, but you're the last to be seated so your looking like what? And now you really wanna stand, no that's okay I don't need to sit.

All had seemed to somehow just get all messed up, somewhere before all this drama and more drama kept coming "daughter" had lost her virginity then down the line somewhere in between 'mothers" intuition started kicking in putting things together from the past connecting to now and instead of here comes the bride, here comes the baby. Yes, "daughter" is pregnant. Okay so long story short "mother" lost it for a minute who is he oh what name did I call him, like it was his fault alone, well actually "mother" lost it for a couple of months maybe about the 4th month I came out of the depressive state. I could not understand how did 'daughter" become pregnant surely two females can not make a baby daa but now this was soo CONFUSING but of course "daughter" was saying she was no longer involved in that lifestyle and they had broken up. This still is more confusion how did you, when did you loose your virginity and who is he how come your family have not met him. If this was not my "daughter" I would have been like how the young people say girl bye and walked away and not come back. Finally "mother"listened to God and others who were trying to say God is the one who creates life, there are no mistakes in God only we make mistakes, because "mother" had shut it down but knew it could not be for long. I began to slowly focus eventually on the prenatal care, doctor visits, eating properly and getting rest and by the 4th month of the pregnancy I was out of denial. It seemed soon as "mother" had come out of denial the devil was up to his old tricks "daughter" started staying out all night pregnant and for about 2 months in the pregnancy moved out. Gone two months living God only knows where for real then before you know it again back home. Well 9 months surely went by really fast and I was glad when on August 2, 2006 I saw my grandson being born, Mr. Jai'yon Malachi Jackson whom I lovingly call Nonnie's boy. So now I am Nonnie instead of Grandma, or nana. He's everybody's baby, his mothers baby, my baby, my mothers baby, my two sisters baby, my cousins baby, right Shanney, he's even my two yr old God daughter's baby. He brought joy, smiles and laughter back to the family, unfortunately "daughter" was back hitting the streets again and he was only a couple of months old or did she ever stop was the question? I started feeling myself getting so close to nonnie's boy and I started trying to pull away to not get close to him but at the same time I had to stay close to keep a watch over him but I was scared to love him so much and be so close and not know if 'daughter' would take him away from me and I couldn't see him. He had been born with two medical conditions that would require possible surgery when God supernaturally healed him of one of them and God brought him successfully through the other one. On the same day of the surgery he was acting like he had just gotten an award for world's happiest baby he was not even cranky or crying. Trips to the hospital in the very beginning of his life were frequent we knew were attacks the 1st trip was a very bad cold for a newborn, the 2nd trip was bronchioleitis, needing breathing treatments, while getting treatments "daughter" is getting phone calls back to back that lead her into this jumpy, antsy, ants in the pants, can't sit still frenzy, and it lead her right out without really saying a word

of the Emergency Room for 45 minutes as "mother" thought she went to get better reception on the phone or something you just gone leave the baby with his grandmother and where the heck you going. All to often this seen before behavior was very familiar, my family and I often say that lifestyle is so scandalous, "daughter" was acting like a person on drugs needing to get a fix or hit, it also made her paranoid, day dream, sneak, lie, looking straight crazy instead of scared straight, weight loss etc.. I mean she would use text messaging like there's no tomorrow or text messaging so fast not evening looking it was almost unbelievable. So while she was gone the nurse in the ER showed me how to give Nonnie boy his treatments. Yeah "daughter" finally came back running down the street looking like a flying nun, with some off the wall excuse about moving the car. Well actually the 3rd trip to the hospital was an admission for 3days with multiple test, injections, medications, fever, monitoring around the clock, and on the 1st night there "daughter" wanted to leave for a while to change clothes.

For what? Your newborn is in the hospital and you don't need clothes if your not going anywhere, don't you want to stay by your baby's side? I was not falling for that she wanted to go make a run. It was like running to the crack house to buy crack cocaine she wanted to run to the house where she could be around the people who hung out in this house and that was basically people in that lifestyle that lived in and out of that particular house. Once nonnie boy was out of the hospital it was still either she would say she was going to the store and stay for hours, or if she took him she would keep him late night hours out. I remember one time my mother was in the hospital and I had to beg her to go to the hospital, I had to pick her up from another house that she hung out at with people in that lifestyle she was all over the place and I waited and waited outside for the longest. When I would confront "daughter" and tell her that the lifestyle was destroying her life, she would laugh in my face and sometimes leave the house as she watched the tears run down my face, still laughing. This would either make me cry harder or get mad on different occasions I had to remember the scripture, "For the weapons of our warfare are not carnal but mighty through God, to the pulling down of strongholds; II Corinthians 10:4, (KJV) and "For we wrestle not against flesh and blood, but against principalities, against powers, against the rulers of the darkness of this world, against spiritual wickedness in high places, Ephesians 6:10 (KJV). These scriptures became and still are my safeguard in God, my defensive weapons because it tells the believer WE have to use Gods word so that it works against the unseen and it does work yes God word does because every time I used the word "daughter" either would flee or shut up or shut down. The behavior It would rise back up again and I would feel like the woman in the bible who's daughter was grieviously vexed with a devil. "And, behold, a woman of Canaan came out of the same coasts, and cried unto him, (*Jesus*) italic mine, saying, Have mercy on me, O Lord, thou Son of David; my daughter is grievously vexed with a devil". Matthew 15:22 (KJV). If this woman who was not of the faith could believe Jesus to heal her daughter and this woman sounded pretty desperate to me, how much more should I a woman of faith be MORE desperate to believe that Jesus would hear my cry for my "daughter" and now there's another life involved her son. When things seem to get worst and it seems like I'm about to loose my JOY I spend my time with Nonnie's BOY!!!!

Phase 7
* A Liar Never Tells the Truth *

Living a lie can't be easy for a liar because you have to tell another lie to cover each lie you tell so that your always lying good God a mighty! I would have to keep my joy full abiding in Jesus and making my own self laugh when I wanted to cry. These lies became "daughters" M-O. So after giving birth although God has a plan for all of our lives. 'Daughter" thought she would plan I guess that she would have her son and her girlfriend who she was back involved with or never even broke up with be like his father what kind of foolishness is that. So now the lie surface from the deep in the letter or some nonsense wrote on paper of baby names and how can you give a baby a woman's last name oh so her goes the lie of the devil "lets get married" ha ha devil that will never happen" mother" thought in the her spirit as she read this crazy letter oh yeah of course mother was snooping again. Eventually "mother" did stop the snooping. You will never get that to happen devil "mother" started talking back to this devil because he was really going to far I'm about to bust this bubble and it will not be nice. So 'mother" confronts daughter who says that old #1lie oh that was a game, are you serious the devil don't play games he puts out hit list, death warrants, he hardly is not playing. When in all actuality mornings, days, and nights of multiple lies of this cover up of two women playing mommy and daddy well that's not a game but the devil wants to make it a lifetime commitment like a man and woman but the devil plays for keeps to win your soul to hell is his ultimate plan. He tries to have a plan like God has a plan for your life but all the devil can do is lie so the people he uses begin to lie. Well "daughter" gets busted being seen with the baby and the suppose to be a young lady acting looking and dressing like a man oh this is not a family affair this is all a lie. "Daughter" wants to say we are friends and she wants to be in the baby's life because the baby dad is not around which that was another situation. Oh ok so "mother" knows that trick "mother" is not so saved holier than thou that she don't know the game the game is the game it's just the devil changes the players from love between a girl and boy to a girl and girl, pictures on facebook that the devil is using girls to show themselves in pictures all hugged up all over each other like it's a lovely thing so people are calling or texting "mother" about did you see or hear but of course "daughter" denies and lies and the proof is right there, also saints of God stop telling stuff and pray talking bout did you see. So okay now weeks and months go by and "daughter" is I can imagine a little tired of the lies so I better just move back out oh or is it the force of the other party saying we can better make it if we live together we grown do your own thing get your mom out your business. So now "mother" is stronger and wiser and so much better now thanks for the lyrics Pastor Marvin Sapp well you know what go ahead go, because when they get tired they'll kick you and the baby out and your family will be waiting with open arms it's just a matter of time, the arguing the confusion, the lies on that end and back home you will come. Of course while "daughter" was out there still, nonnie's boy not knowing what was going on from one place to the other one environment to the other covered in prayer. Well a year does go by "daughter" did get put out or she left and the baby is 1yrs old we made a year hal-le-uah! For the baby to have his 1st birthday party. "Daughter" is finally at the end of a thing how and when God does a thing all the time we can't always tell. We just know he does it and you can see and feel it coming to an end. Or sometimes you don't you just know there is change we hear the saying often he may not come when you want him but he's right on time. You just know attitude, heart has changed, hair is back healthy skin is clearer, weight picks up actions are louder than words now. In the end a lie won't stand but the truth will prevail.

Phase 8
Victory Is Always Sweet

V is for vindicator
I is for in, in God
C is for control
T is for time
O is for order
R is for ready
Y is for you

When God is ready for you and you have been called out for him and by him the victory is always sweet the process is bitter but that time will be as a moment in time that it took it seems soo forever but that moment was so all worth it all that for this moment is grand, what a grand slam home run . By none other not the baseball league but our God! Don't know when don't know how but "daughter" was back home and out, did you read what "mother" just wrote out I mean out in the name of Jesus. This time it was no more games, lies, struggling, back and forth it was a wrap a done deal. See when God does it, it is completed it is signed and sealed in his name and his blood. The cross was bitter but the resurrection was sweet with victory. There was literally a cross that stayed in my bedroom that the Holy Spirit had me make it was a old wood cross that stood to my knee caps to represent when 'daughter" was a baby and to remember the things about her as a baby and promises God had given down the years in her life. There was red writing on the cross of course red writing representing Jesus blood his words of instruction to me was to write the word homosexuality and lesbianism is nailed to the cross with drops of blood, a picture of my daughter and the scripture Proverbs 11:21(KJV)Though hand join in hand, the wicked shall not be unpunished: but the **seed** of the **righteous** shall be delivered to show that it is written. I would meditate quote and believe those words with all my heart because God said if you do I will surely bring it to pass she will be totally healed delivered and free and come home. It took a year or so of praying before those words in that one scripture became alive active and operating but God had never lied when he spoke that it never left mother's heart in the most difficult despairing times. That cross was so special because it reminded me of what Jesus died for and how my obedience to hear the Holy Spirit to do something my human mind could not think to do. I would place the cross in such a safe place keeping and covered when I would have guess because it was for no one to see besides me and him. Through all the bitter pain the sweetness rested in the victory of it all would be over one day and mother would see it. It gave such a comfort to hear those that spoke its just a matter of time, she's coming out, God is gone do it I have no doubt about that, keep holding on don't give up!...The amazing awesomeness of God is that when we he does it and you don't even really realize he's done it because you did not see this big elaborate thing happen or you did not hear this testimony of step by step but oh how he just showed up and you just know one day you were freed your cries and prayers were answered and you can't even explain the substance of what you had been hoping for. Sounds like faith to me! If we endure and hold out he's coming into your situation if you want it and trust him and except his ever loving help through all the pain after the pain your victory will await you, he will not, not show up and give you the freedom you desire but it must be a desire, to be tasted. Victory is only won after you have fought in the battle you must put up your dukes in the spirit and fight, the battle is the Lords but your own will must be conquered by your own allowance to let your will be conquered and your participation in your victory celebration. During the celebration does the enemy hang around no not for the celebration but he will usually show back up and lurk around but as he see that God has truly delivered even he goes away and realize that he has loss. He knows that a victory against God he could never win.

Phase 9
* Determined to Do Damage to Darkness *

It was always the plan of God for daughter and mother to work and be in ministry together this is why mother could never give up and mother had to do ministry or should I say kingdom work as a team. The kingdom of God must be done in earth as it is in heaven. As God begin to launch mother into prayer for those that are battling in this area the anointing of God just always showed up and God would do the work, mother would only just be the vessel or the vehicle. People would be healed delivered set free and understand that the yoke that was on them was broken praise God to him belong and get the glory only. For mother it would be foolishness and too much time and energy on her own. Daughter began to voluntarily or should I say it really was God's plan to be a armor bearer for mother every time mother had to preach out daughter was there and determined to watch as well as pray that darkness would be exposed and destroyed not just in this area but whatever was taking place in that place or in that atmosphere like on a night of a revival. God had us joined at the hip as a team to help us to help his people. We would see the same things feel the same things in the realm of the spirit as God guided us and showed us how to effectively do what he called for in that assignment or call. It was truly a reward from heaven it was glorious as he would also minister to the both of us together or individually and we would come back with the same thing. Daughter would sing and others would say that her voice was so angelic, she was singing since she was 3 years old and she knew if she was at service with mother, she was going to ask her to sing, her singing would bring such an light into the atmosphere that if there was any darkness it would half to lighten up. The enemy never wants the light to shine on the dark areas of our lives or those we are connected to or God wants us to connect with. So he will always keep the blinders and scales so thick that no light can get in it will just be pitched black dark. However the anointing would bring the power of light to break forth because it shines in the darkest of the dark places of the heart. This was not just about this only it was for something else and someone else it was for us to be delivered in other areas as well and to help others in this or in something else. There was a time when the power of God fell on daughter just being in the presence of God's spirit that was on mother and there was a impartation of his presence that daughter hit the floor and God's presence and voice began to hoover over her as he was giving her more than she expected.. The turn around in her life lead her to want to begin to pray again and seek him again for her life like how when she was 11yrs old and now for her son. She began to allow her light in her to show the darkness in her friends who God is and was in her life from a little girl. There began to be a wanting and longing to change for her friends who now wanted to experience change and the light, this would do damage to the darkness that they were in because now they can come into the light of Jesus in a dark world and because the darkness could not comprehend light. Mother and daughter began to do mini bible study with friends and even invite them to services of healing and deliverance where the devil could be cast out. There was a time of going to the floor of prayer (threshing floor) where the spirit of the Lord visited the both of us mother always knew she had things to do for God but she knew it could not get going without daughter and we were engulfed with a prayer sheet wrapped about us that carried God's anointing and as we were laying in his presence we didn't even know how long. He spoke to both of us as we were both in his presence and was later able to share his awesomeness of how he spoke to us to help each other and help others.

We both knew we could not do anything without each other and definitely without God for this particular ministry that requires us together as he has given us double portion anointing.

Why did I write the book?

Why did I write this book? I didn't the Holy Spirit did, I not only would have ever thought of or wanted to write a book ESPECIALLY on this topic of lesbianism never this because while it seems to help some to see the light of truth through the word of God it hurts others who don't believe that or see that the bible speaks against it. I felt all hope was lost and gone for my daughter and that's when the Holy Spirit spoke to me to write about it this was even before she came out. I was told by a person in the church that's a hard spirit to break and that they knew of someone that died in that lifestyle which discouraged me and kind of deadened my hope for ay first to write about my experience or believe that she would one day come out of it. Then I was told by another person in the church that they really didn't know how to help me and by their honesty I was shocked but it was I guess their honesty and later I understood as God sent people to pray with me and for my daughter to under gird us and believe God for anything. God begin to show me that the church is a building and people are human but the church is in you, you are the church and that as Jesus says up on this rock I will build my church and the very gates of hell would not prevail against it, that was powerful. This began to push me to pray more and pray more fervent!. I remember one day trying to do things in my own strength God spoke to me and said you cannot save your daughter you don't have the power to save only my word has the power to save and you can never do what my word can. He told me my word is in her she knows my word the word will get it done against all odds. Once I realized it was an assignment and a ministry I remembered a favorite movie of mine called not without my daughter that moved me and inspired me that this movie would be the title of my book. There is always purpose that can be found in when you have experienced something and you can help someone else who may have had your same problem or if you have overcome a battle that most would say it's a no way no win situation and then you win you are able to help and show others that winning is possible. Through the word of God, prayer, and the way of God's instruction in the bible. I was excited and happy to take the challenge, risk, and stand to help the lost and the saved, the believer, the non-believer, the person that cares and the person that does not care. No matter what age, sex, race color or creed it does and did not matter I just knew that I had a determined will through the power of God's word again against all odds against me to say daughter I don't care what you say, feel, do, or think you will not out win or beat God's word. I guarantee you that. It would be a fight through prayer and God's word that I would use to help me fight not with a fist, weapon or words in the natural human argumentive language but in the Spirit of God. I didn't want to debate or prove I just wanted God to perform his word through me for her. I wanted to show the devil if I am to have a purpose that I must fulfill for my life in the kingdom of God then I knew my seed had to have a greater purpose and it was up to me to protect the seed God had given me with greater purpose. So I would not just do all that God had for me and not prepare the next generation after me I knew I could not even go into ministry alone without what God had already shown me he had begun in her. He had started a work in her and he had allowed me to see it to partake of it to be blessed by it and I knew He God had begun a good work in her as well as myself and we would be a team and he would complete the work he started in her. So I could not go on without her. I did not want to be a person who goes to church and didn't take her child I wanted all the blessings of God and what I learned and had benefited from for her to reap those same benefits and blessings as I received I wanted for her. I wanted the pain I felt to maybe feel less for someone else that could read this book church or non-church and say I can identify or if not identify totally but maybe get a hope or get a feel to see things in another way another light of love. I wanted to embrace all ethnicity and say or give a voice, a message of hope, change of mind and thinking even if slowly but surely. Not to not understand that emotions are emotions feelings are feelings and they are real but we must ask God to allow his word God's word to internalize in us to help us understand that God's word through prayer openness and the Holy Spirit can help our emotions and feelings that dominate us to react but to his word. To overcome our will and emotions so we can do what's right not what we feel is right there is a difference. It is like in the natural a father in the natural a good father knows what's best for his child although the child think he knows what is best because of what he or she feels or wants but the parent is the parent for a reason. So like God he knows what is best for us when we cannot see or understand it that way, we want our way or what we feel but God knows and wants to speak from the bible but will he have those that will listen and consider. It is a challenge, it is a battle, it is a struggle, it is a law that says its okay but the evidence is proven in God's word that it is not. If I could be used by God to help others, as well as my daughter then it is worth the controversy. I was determined to see her out and tell about it and write about it. I wanted to write about it so that where there is darkness on this matter there would be a light shining to expose the dark area to bring a light of hope one of the reasons why some stay in the closet is because they are not only ashamed and embarassed on the matter but deep down they question is this really right or wrong. Then when some come out of the closet they have convinced themselves through feelings and emotions and love this is what I want and who I am emotions feelings and our love does not define or validate who we are God word does. He only knows the plans and thoughts of our lives, our emotions can have us loving today hating tomorrow but God's word does not change it speaks, settles, and establishes what is suppose to be.

To all young girls:

You are wonderfully and beautifully made by God. You are God's princess's and his precious gifts. Diamonds, pearls, jewels, rubies and roses. You are all of different ethnicity, skin color, shapes, sizes, heights, weights, hairstyles, long, short, curly, natural, kinky, straight, thin or thick and all of that is special. God knows your hurts, of trauma pain, disappointments, low-self esteem, the break up of a boyfriend, the absent of a father who was never there or you don't even know, God knows the peer pressures in your school, life, or even in your family, he knows the name calling, the bullying, the picking, the harassment. Those of you that have been violated by rape, molestation, mental emotional abuse, verbal abuse, physical abuse, from inside your family, a friend of family, or by a total stranger. God knows terrible, horrible, events have happened in your life and HE wants to HEAL you and let you through this love letter to you through me HE is saying I love you and you were not made to be boy or to be with another girl for NO REASON. I love everything about you and I am so sorry for all the pain, hurt, and disappoint you had happen to you. I did not like all that stuff that happened to you and I am sorry for those who have hurt and disappointed you those have done these things to you. I am here now for you in and through this love letter to let you know I want to take away and help and ease your pain you can tell me and talk to me God is saying. I will help you hold your hand and help you understand and get you through this the same way I did with "daughter" in this book just as she is my daughter so are you, let me see you through this now. I am sorry about the past but let me help you for your better future how I did with 'daughter" invite me into your heart in the midnight hour when you are all alone or in whatever the hour is that you need me. I will never be busy or turn you away I will always have time for you, and you can count on me and trust right now even as you read your love letter. I won't judge you or hurt you in any way NEVER.

From the Author to the Gay/Lesbian Community

It is with great sympathy and empathy that I write to you not to condemn any of you I have no right or power to do that but to sincerely say that I apologize if this book hurt or offends you. As I have said through the entire book I love you as God does and I embrace you. I did not set out to offend or attack you I am not against any of you how could I say that I am a Christian and hate you, Christ came and died for all and for love but there is always standards that must be set, I set out to stand on the truth of the Holy scriptures that I cannot deny it is not my words or feelings it is his words precisely spoken. I can't take part of the word of God and not the other parts that offend I must take the whole bible from beginning to end even if it hurts or offends me. It hurts me if I have hurt anyone and it hurts me if I have hurt some or all of you by this book but sometimes things in the bible hurt me to. However I would rather be hurt, get and know the real truth get healed then to reject and not know the truth and find out later and have to pay, for later it was I came to realize that the truth was presented to me and I didn't take it. I know a lot of you are in relationships right now or even marriages and feel like who is she I am not breaking up with my significant other I am not divorcing my spouse some of you may say I have been this way all my life all I can say is God will do the severing, with love, restoring and healing. God will never like a surgeon separate you and not put you back together to your proper state, order or condition. For those that are single I pray that you will pray to stay single and be freed and healed "Buy the truth and sell it not"

Love you ALL

Printed in the United States
By Bookmasters